LEAD
WELL

PAULA DAVIS, JD, MAPP

LEAD WELL

5 MINDSETS
TO ENGAGE, RETAIN, AND INSPIRE YOUR TEAM

WHARTON
SCHOOL
PRESS
Philadelphia

Published by
Wharton School Press
An Imprint of University of Pennsylvania Press
3905 Spruce Street
Philadelphia, Pennsylvania 19104-4112
wsp.wharton.upenn.edu

Printed in the United States of America on acid-free paper
10   9   8   7   6   5   4   3   2   1

Ebook ISBN: 9781613631904
Paperback ISBN: 9781613631898

To Lucy, you are my greatest teacher and my favorite human

Contents

Introduction

When I was eight and my brother was five, my dad left his steady-paycheck, full-time job at a large dairy manufacturer to pursue his side hustle. He purchased a plastic injection molding company and, at the time, had just two small molding machines and one client. His "office" was an old hog barn located on a friend's property just outside of town in rural Wisconsin, and it was anything but fancy. His first "employee" was a feral cat named Tiger.

It was a bold move with no guarantees, and the early years were hard—and lean. Our car was an $840 piece of junk (I'm being kind) and during the summer we traveled the Midwest, eating peanut butter and jelly sandwiches my mom made, while my dad made sales calls just hoping to make enough money to pay the bills. For the first few years, my dad worked nonstop, which meant my mom was responsible for all the parenting, household chores, and school activities. She said it was stressful having to wear so many hats by herself, and on top of that, her mom (my grandmother) became very sick during that time.[1]

My dad endured many sleepless nights and constant sales calls with no leads; he wondered many times whether he made the wrong decision. I asked what kept him going, and he said that he was young, energetic, and he just kept hoping that the next lead would turn into something. The uncertainty tested both of my parents' resilience and resolve.

The turning point came five years into his business, when a large window manufacturer fired their parts supplier and gave some of the work to my dad. My dad, always a man of his word and brilliant at building relationships, nurtured this new connection. He delivered parts at all hours of the day and night, making sure that the company never had to shut down a line due to lack of product. My dad called it "extreme client service." They rewarded my dad with more business, yet my dad knew he couldn't rely on just one client. He continued to pursue other leads and eventually, that turned into more work.

Over the years, the business grew, eventually expanding into a three-shift operation, housed in a large manufacturing building. His employees were loyal, and that was important. Working in a plastic injection molding company isn't easy work. It's repetitive, boring at times, loud, and extremely hot in the summer.

My dad didn't go to college and has no formal business training other than what he learned in his various jobs. I wanted to know more about how he figured out how to do all of this, so I asked him about his leadership philosophy (which made him laugh) and how he managed to build a culture that felt like family. He told me about a managerial position he had with a large company, where he and others were treated poorly, very frequently and very publicly. He never forgot it, and so he knew that he wanted people to truly enjoy their work.

He treated everyone with respect (one of my dad's core values), and he expected his shift managers to follow suit. And he extended that respect to everyone, regardless of title or position. He also wanted people to feel keenly appreciated, so he paid them a fair wage, said thank you a lot, and had pizza and donut "parties." Over time, working there felt like community. I remember the first-shift material handler grilling out and hosting impromptu picnics for all the employees from time to time.

When my dad asked people to do tough tasks, like change out a heavy mold in 100+ degree heat, he would often do the work right alongside, as a way to say, "I'm in this with you." He knew that if he treated people with dignity and respect, they would not only pay it forward, but they would also rise to the occasion and help during tough times. And they did.

Beyond simply building a business based on his values, my dad is a paragon of social intelligence and relationship building. Several of the young salespeople and executives who worked with my parents grew in their careers right alongside my dad. When my parents sold the business, they said the hardest thing to leave behind was the relationships. One of the salespeople told me years ago that my dad is the finest man he has encountered in all his travels. I have fond memories of my time working in the business, and we all still reminisce about it frequently.

My dad's journey illustrates what this book is about. Resilience, values alignment, appreciation, connection, community (and more) are foundational elements for building and leading an amazing culture. What my dad instinctively knew back in 1983 has become the new leadership imperative today.

Beyond Burnout: A New Leadership Competency

I have made it my life's work to better understand the psychological impact of stress and how it affects and influences individuals, leaders, and teams at work. I explored the topic of burnout prevention in my first book, *Beating Burnout at Work: Why Teams Hold the Secret to Well-Being and Resilience* (2021). It was not only a topic I studied and taught through my organization, but it was also something I knew about firsthand because I had experienced burnout myself.

I suspected that the conversation about burnout needed to be expanded—that it needed to be talked about also as a systemic, culture-influenced problem, and the research supported that position. And as I talked to leaders and teams about what caused their stress, I discovered that systemic and culture-influenced factors appeared in every conversation. The work environment impacts individuals, leaders, and teams in many ways, but it's not traditionally how we've approached the burnout and workplace well-being conversation.

This book is the unexpected outgrowth of the ways in which these conversations have helped me reframe how to make work better. While I have been doing this work for more than a decade, from 2020 to 2023 I taught nearly 400 workshops, trainings, keynotes, and programs on burnout prevention, building resilient teams, and other related well-being, positive psychology, and leadership-focused programs. During this period, the leaders and teams with whom I worked helped me realize how we've missed the mark.

Legacy Approaches to Managing Teams & Well-Being Are Outdated

There is a knowledge gap in how to educate leaders and teams about these topics, so leaders fall back on legacy approaches ("This is the way we've always done it"). Many leaders are undereducated about the foundational skills involved with making a job more meaningful, how to apply science-based tools to leverage high performance, how to create close communities at work, and the sources of intrinsic motivation. Because of this, they have very little idea about specific short-term and long-term strategies that will truly engage, retain, and inspire their teams, and these concepts are not often taught in leadership training programs.

A "Me and a We" Approach Is a Must

While the pandemic opened the door to a much-needed and more robust conversation about mental health and well-being, most organizations approached the ensuing stress as exclusively an individual problem, which led to an overemphasis on individual-focused, one-size-fits-all tactics that didn't solve for the root causes of chronic stress and burnout in the first place.

My conversations with leaders and teams about these root causes exposed the sore spots and unresolved issues they regularly faced and led us to explore issues like culture, teaming practices and processes, workload, and the deeper conversations that were needed but weren't being had.

In addition, I noticed that leaders often disconnected the human aspects of work from the performance aspects of work. As a result, leaders often chose to prioritize performance above people and/or viewed well-being as just an HR thing and not a leadership competency to be developed.[2] To help, organizations must take a "me and a we" approach that focuses both on how individuals can continue to help themselves thrive (the "me") *and* what leaders can do to create a better environment in which to make thriving more likely (the "we"). There needs to be a much greater emphasis placed on the "we," and leaders drive this conversation.

Short-Term Thinking Stalls Many Efforts in This Space

As you will see from the stories and case studies I share in this book, making work better takes time. I understand that you may report to leaders, executives, and boards that require to you take a short-term, bottom-line, business focus, but that short-termism needs to be balanced with the longer-term people side. Both need to be thought of in parallel and promoted equally.

Leaders Need Simple Tools & a Clear Path Forward

While I believe that many leaders truly want to help their teams thrive, they are uncertain about where to start and how to identify and assess the issues driving the problem. In addition, leaders need to better understand the psychological, emotional, well-being, and bottom-line consequences of working in a state of constant change and uncertainty. Unfortunately, many managers and leaders are stressed themselves, and they are trying to effectively lead teams that are also exhausted. They need simple and effective tools to help.

Why Now? 4 Factors Impacting Our Experience of Work

In addition to what I learned, there have recently been macro-level changes to work that have also had consequences for people and teams. We are living in a time of great challenge and great opportunity. Leading well requires that leaders have a keen understanding of the following four factors.

Factor 1: The Pandemic Altered Our Collective Perspective about Work & Life

The pandemic was an upheaval event that impacted literally everyone on the planet. During this time, many people were scared, chronically stressed, overwhelmed, and frustrated. Upheaval events amplify people's search for meaning and purpose. Post-traumatic growth (PTG) is the experience of positive change after going through a significantly stressful event. Researchers have discovered five common themes that people tend to report after experiencing a significantly stressful event:[3]

- Renewed appreciation for life
- Enhanced personal strength
- Stronger, more meaningful relationships
- Spiritual growth
- Recognizing new paths for your life

It's important to note that PTG doesn't mean people emerge unscathed from the experience. Many, if not most, strongly wish the event hadn't happened and may still be in pain. While it's hard to estimate the prevalence of PTG, it's far from being an unusual or rare phenomenon and may explain, in part, why so many people are searching for meaning, purpose, and a deep sense of mattering both at work and outside of work post-pandemic.

For many people, the pandemic created a once-in-a-lifetime opportunity to try something new, sometimes in a big and transformative way. We all learned that tomorrow is not promised, so why not do what matters now?

Factor 2: Uncertainty & Instability Are the Norm

Leaders must recognize that big shifts are changing how people work. According to a *McKinsey Quarterly* report, "The climate crisis, global health challenges, and changes in social values are upending individual priorities. Globalization and geopolitics are shifting the world's tectonic plates. How we live and work is being constantly reinvented by advances in technology and the emergence of generations who were 'born digital.'"[4] In addition, rapid advances in technology are forcing organizations to transform at an unprecedented pace and frequency.

At the same time, people analytics leader David Green noted that "companies are confronted with a series of organizational shifts that have significant implications for structures, processes, and people. These include complex questions around finding an optimal balance between in-person and remote work, building new organizational capabilities in the face of challenging (and changing) workforce demographics and talent gaps, and focusing on developing a healthy, inclusive, and thriving company culture."[5] These types of changes (both large and small, acute and ongoing) create psychological pressure and strain in unexpected ways and continue to drive stress and exhaustion.

There are important employee well-being implications that stem from uncertainty, especially prolonged uncertainty. Uncertainty kicks off a process that causes people at work to scan their environment for safety cues. Employees ask themselves: Does management have a plan in place? Are leaders telling us what's happening? Do I believe the accuracy of the information I'm being told? When the answer is no, anxiety rises, and over time, being in a prolonged anxious state leads to exhaustion.[6]

Volatility, change, and uncertainty will continue to define work for the foreseeable future; however, change and instability often strengthen workers' resolve to find and advocate for well-being, meaning, and work-life balance, reinforcing Factor 1.[7]

Factor 3: A Technology-Enabled Future Will Require a Human-Centered Leadership Approach

People and technology will need to coexist. Generative AI (GenAI) is in the process of transforming certain aspects of work, and this will only accelerate as the technology becomes more sophisticated and organizations learn more about how to use it and how it is being used. As a result, it's critical for teams to think about what's possible for humans in the age of GenAI. Employers will need to be educators on both GenAI tools *and* people skills. Leaders must now know how to lead in a way that promotes community, creativity, communication, teamwork, and other human-focused qualities that GenAI tools will have a difficult time replicating. In addition, human-centered skills will live on and persist in ways that hard skills cannot, potentially making them more important than ever.[8]

Factor 4: Leaders Need to Incorporate Practices That Amplify Meaningful Work & Promote Values Alignment

People want more than a paycheck from work. They want their values to align with their organization's values, and they want their leaders to walk the talk. They want a sense of purpose and meaning in their work, and leaders need to be able to connect the dots to this higher level of aspiration. While meaning and values alignment are important generally, they are critical work must-haves for Millennials and Gen Z.

The How: A Blueprint to Help Teams Thrive

Great leadership has always been needed for companies to grow and to thrive, but the "how" of going about it has changed. If you want to solve for the well-being challenges that exist at work today, then you need to think differently and educate your leaders and teams accordingly. The combination of factors I have outlined above has psychological, emotional, well-being, and bottom-line consequences for the workplace. This combination has permanently changed our relationship with work, and there is no going back. We can't unsee or unlive the flexibility that might have been afforded to us during the pandemic and what that meant for how we lived and worked. We won't soon forget the social isolation and loneliness that also impacted so many during the pandemic.

This book represents a summary of my hundreds of conversations with thousands of leaders and employees, boosted by what the latest in psychological science suggests everyone must know about how to thrive in today's world of work and adapt to change. The book offers leaders a blueprint to follow that will give them the tools to have the right conversation to (1) address the root causes of stress and motivation; (2) build thriving teams that stay engaged, connected, and inspired; and (3) help their teams adapt to and navigate change, complexity, and uncertainty. Collectively, I call this approach "Lead Well," and have crafted five mindsets for leaders to develop:

- Mindset #1: Prioritize Sticky Recognition & Mattering
- Mindset #2: Amplify ABC Needs
- Mindset #3: Create Workload Sustainability
- Mindset #4: Build Systemic Stress Resilience
- Mindset #5: Promote Values Alignment & Meaning

Part I of the book establishes why work isn't working and presents the new approach that is required. Chapter 1 explains the serious challenges we're facing and lays out a powerful business case for the Lead Well mindsets. Chapter 2 looks at both the root causes of chronic stress and disengagement and the root causes of motivation and high performance—the positive upside that must be leveraged by leaders. It goes into greater depth on why taking a "me and we" approach is necessary.

Part II shifts focus and explores the Lead Well mindsets that will help leaders create an environment to engage, retain, and inspire their teams. Chapter 3 talks about the first mindset—creating sticky recognition and mattering. "Sticky" recognition is a phrase I coined to help leaders identify feedback that shows individuals and teams the evidence of their impact, a critical element that makes recognition stick. Sticky recognition leads to mattering, a powerful state where people know they are both achieving important goals and feeling valued.

Chapter 4 unpacks the second mindset—prioritizing ABC needs (autonomy, belonging, and challenge). These are a powerful trio that form the basis of intrinsic motivation and fuel engagement, high performance, and thriving at work. You can also think about this trio as the combination of flexibility, connection, and continuous growth. ABC needs form the foundation of several workplace health and well-being frameworks.

Chapter 5 is about the third mindset—workload sustainability.[9] Leaders are often stuck and frustrated about how to manage team workloads, yet they acknowledge that it's a huge source of stress for their teams and prevents work-life integration. A 2024 American Psychological Association survey found that only 40% of respondents said that their time off is respected.[10] People need to be allowed some time to detach and fully recharge and recover so they can bring their best selves to work. This includes leaders and managers too.

Chapter 6 explores the importance of systemic stress resilience—the fourth mindset. In an uncertain and complex world, humans face a tremendous number of challenges, both big and small. GenAI alone has raised the uncertainty stakes about how work gets done. And more generally, leaders and teams need to be able to make critical, real-time decisions as new information is learned and contexts shift. Resilience is about capacity and growth, and individuals, leaders, teams, and organizations will need it in spades given the uncertain and complex path leading to the future of work.

Lastly, leaders need to amplify and reestablish values alignment and meaning in work—the fifth mindset, which I discuss in chapter 7. There I'll talk about new research that identifies six key practices leaders can develop to increase meaning at work and realign values.

I'll conclude with recommendations for implementation, and I will direct you to specific resources that will help support your success.

To set you up for success as you read the book, please note that all the tools, techniques, skills, and ideas are flagged as Tiny Noticeable Things (TNTs™). Many of the TNTs can be implemented very quickly, while others take a bit more time, reflection, and discussion. They are research-based, and many have been road-tested successfully in my workshops. Also, many of the TNTs are team-focused. I like to take a teams-based approach to my work. I think these tools are easier to implement and more effective when they are incorporated into each team's unique culture, rather than trying to change an entire culture collectively. My hope is that you discuss the TNTs with your own teams and implement them together based on your specific stressors. Lastly, the chapters are supported by case studies and stories from industry leaders, stories from my workshops, and ideas from noted researchers. I hope that they inspire you to see how these mindsets and ideas are being implemented.

After the widespread instability and uncertainty that we have all recently experienced, the time is now for leaders to think differently and to Lead Well. It's an opportunity to shape the way teams thrive in the future of work, so that everyone is better equipped and empowered to navigate the disruptions and opportunities yet to come.

PART I

**A New Approach to Work
Is Needed**

Chapter 1

Creating a Human-Centered Future

Jay Shah had a critical decision to make.[11] In 2009, Jay was the chief information officer and part of the original team that launched Personal Capital's wealth management platform, a cutting-edge technology company in the financial sector. The fintech start-up grew in the decade that followed, and, as 2020 approached, a company expressed interest in acquiring the business. Jay, then the president and CEO of Personal Capital, was excited about what this next chapter held. As his team proceeded through the due diligence process to ready the company for sale, what they didn't expect was the onset of a global pandemic. Jay told me that over the course of a few tense days, his team was divided on what approach to take as the pandemic gained steam. Half of his senior team felt that it was critical to remain in the office to maintain important business functions and continuity, which they knew might be critical to advancing the sale. The other half felt strongly that the entire company should be allowed to work from home to protect employee health and safety, even if it meant that the result might be losing the sale.

When the senior team could not reach a consensus, Jay made the decision to allow everyone to work from home. In the days that followed, he emphasized the importance of close communication (the senior team stayed connected via continuous virtual conversations), data-driven decision making, and taking a pragmatic approach to overcoming fear and division within the senior team. As the team started to stabilize and align, they realized that the challenges they faced were based more on fear than actual concrete obstacles. In August 2020, Personal Capital closed on its sale to Empower.

What allowed Jay to be decisive in such a critical moment was a reliance on values—not just his own, but also what the company had identified as its compass for good behavior. Jay emphasized that the decision was a people decision, not a business one, which had the potential to positively impact the business in the long run. It's probably fair to say that few leaders anticipated the deeply disruptive nature of the pandemic and the speed with which organizations would therefore have to adapt and transform themselves. As it turns out, one of the most critical aspects of organizational health is decisive and empowering decision making—how leaders operate day-to-day and lead their teams.[12] The pandemic tested leaders' decision making and so much more.

How the Pandemic Changed Work

The pandemic disrupted labor markets around the world in 2020, and it did so sharply and suddenly. Within weeks, millions of people were laid off or lost their jobs, while others were forced to rapidly adjust to fully remote work as offices closed.[13] As the days turned into weeks, it became clear that the pandemic was not going to be short-term. Stress and uncertainty climbed as news cycles turned into nonstop death-reporting machines. The pandemic was an upheaval event that, over time, caused many people to reflect on their work and life trajectories, with many making changes to one or both domains after being confronted with the fact that their jobs and/or loved ones could be gone overnight. According to an Indeed survey of US workers who switched jobs at least twice since the start of the pandemic, "92% said that the pandemic made them feel life is too short to stay in a job they weren't passionate about."[14]

This mass exodus of workers became known as the Great Resignation. The Great Resignation first gained momentum in the United States in 2021, when nearly 47.4 million people quit their jobs. Many cited lack of connection to the organization. Work had become transactional, and burnout was increasing, as was grief and exhaustion.

Nearly 4.2 million US workers left their jobs voluntarily in November 2022.[15] And many of the employees who didn't outright quit started to "quiet quit"—they disengaged from their jobs, vowing only to do the bare minimum. Quiet quitting and the Great Resignation were both large-scale responses to people's dissatisfaction with work.

Heading into 2023, more and more people decided that they didn't want to settle for jobs that didn't prioritize their well-being, and expectations of happiness at work increased.[16] While being fairly compensated is typically among the top reasons why employees stay (71% citing pay in one report), having meaningful work matters almost as much (in the same report, 69% said meaning made for a fulfilling job).[17] Other reasons included, "My team cares about my well-being," "I can be creative and innovative in my job," "I can choose when I work," and "I can choose where I work."[18]

Hybrid work forced leaders to rethink and to even reinvent the meaning and experience of their workplace culture.[19] Worker stress has remained at record high levels since the pandemic, and companies must have a clear strategy for protecting people from burnout and addressing mental health issues.[20] Organizations that want to continue to attract and retain top talent will need a clear well-being value proposition. People generally have rethought what work means to them, what they want from life, and how work and life should integrate in a post-pandemic world. Meaning, mattering, and appreciation mean more to people at work than ever before.

A New Challenge: Humans + Machines

As the pandemic eased, another seismic shift to work was waiting— the massive rise of GenAI. While understanding more about GenAI and its capabilities is a top priority right now for many organizations, the conversation about human capital needs to sit right next to it, according to Jen Fisher, former chief wellbeing officer at Deloitte.[21] She challenges leaders to think differently and more long-term about the human capital side of work. She said that companies need to create and invest in long-term strategies for developing thriving teams, much like they already do for finance, operations, and technology.

Marti Wronski, chief operating officer (COO) for the Milwaukee Brewers, a Major League Baseball team based in Milwaukee, Wisconsin, couldn't agree more. One of the things that Marti is most passionate about in her role as COO is helping her team thrive.[22] When I talked to her, she emphasized that taking a bottom-line, business-first "How do we look right now in the moment?" focus is important. But what often gets missed, or excluded and not prioritized, is the long-term play. She said that leaders must also strategize for the ways in which they develop their people over the long term.

Jen and I talked about the enormous risk of getting the GenAI + humans intersection wrong, and the huge opportunity to get it right. The risk is that the more tech-focused companies become, the greater the potential to devalue human-centered skills. On the other hand, GenAI tools could help leaders and teams free up time and capacity, thus presenting an opportunity to shine a light on what humans do well at work—those traits that cannot be replaced by technology.

More generally, as we enter the Fourth Industrial Revolution, work is more complex and uncertain than ever before. And operating at a much faster pace. The McKinsey Global Institute estimates that the pandemic will accelerate occupational transitions by as much as 25%.[23] Workers are moving 25% faster toward job loss, job change, and role change. In addition, symptoms of depression and anxiety are up by as much as 400% since the start of the pandemic, particularly among young adults, communities of color, essential workers, and mothers.[24] Talent retention issues, rising burnout rates, where-to-work conversations, loneliness and making connections, and intergenerational teaming are all huge challenges leaders and organizations face.

Leaders & Employees Are Misaligned

The well-being, happiness, and engagement fallout from these challenges is real. Low engagement costs the global economy $8.9 trillion—9% of the global GDP.[25] In addition, worker stress has remained at a historic high, even as some of the other negative emotional fallout from the pandemic has subsided.[26] A key concern is that leaders seem to be missing this. According to Deloitte's 2023 *Workplace Well-Being* report, 66% of employees said their well-being stayed the same or got worse; yet, more than 75% of executives inaccurately believed their workforce's well-being had improved. And the news wasn't much different in Deloitte's 2024 report. Its research revealed that almost 90% of executives believed that working for their company has a positive impact on skill development, well-being, belonging, and meaning, yet only 60% of workers agreed.[27] Another survey found an average 22% gap between employer and employee perceptions, with employers consistently rating dimensions of well-being more favorably than employees.[28] In addition, employees and leaders are consistently misaligned about what employees cite as being critical to their experience of work (and leaders keep overlooking the importance). Employees have been shown to value six aspects of work more than managers realize: being valued by my manager; being valued by my organization; having caring and trusting teammates; potential for advancement; a sense of belonging; and flexible work schedules.[29]

Even more interesting is that, across the board, 59% of employees, 66% of managers, and 71% of the C-suite reported that they would seriously contemplate taking a job at another company that would better support their well-being.[30] There is clearly a huge disconnect between senior leaders and their employees, even though many senior leaders are experiencing the very same stress, burnout, and low well-being concerns as their teams.

Creating a Healthier Workplace Culture Starts with Leaders

Leaders play a critical role in shaping a workplace environment that leads to employee thriving and well-being. A recent study by the Workforce Institute at UKG revealed that managers have an outsized impact on well-being. When they asked survey respondents who has the greatest impact on their mental health, 41% of respondents said their therapist, 51% said their doctor, and 69% said their manager (on par with the impact of their spouse).[31] In addition, other research showed that compared to colleagues, family, and friends, supervisors were the most important source of support in reducing burnout.[32] Separate research found that a whopping 70% of the variance in team engagement is explained by the manager.[33] However, most leaders are not given the tools, support, or empowerment to make an impact. Heavy workload, unsupportive cultures that promote toxic productivity, and not having the right skills are the main reasons why leaders say they stumble in this area. As a result, only about 40% of managers feel capable of helping their company achieve its well-being commitments.[34]

Even though leaders do face organizational hurdles, there are messages they could send about well-being that are fully within their control to deliver, which they presently are not. Deloitte found that only:

- 54% of leaders check in with their teams to ask how they're doing
- 37% make sure team members use or take their paid time off
- 30% model healthy behaviors
- 26% lead team well-being activities[35]

One of the most effective ways to boost engagement is a process most managers don't use. Researchers discovered that 80% of employees who said they had a meaningful conversation with their manager in the past week were fully engaged—regardless of how many days they worked in the office.[36] Meaningful conversations include some appreciation, clarity of goals and priorities, are short (15–30 minutes is enough), and are strengths-based.[37]

The Business Case: Positive Work Cultures Drive Good Business Outcomes

Some leaders may dismiss the factors associated with developing a positive work culture as soft, but it is a new frontier (and important differentiator) in the competition for talent and is a key ingredient in business success. When companies fail to create an environment where people are less stressed and more engaged, they leave money on the table by choosing not to change. When people feel burned out, overwhelmed, disengaged, disconnected, lonely, overloaded, languishing, or some combination thereof, performance, productivity, motivation, and engagement suffer, and that has bottom-line consequences.

There are significant business outcomes associated with creating a thriving work culture. So what are the economic benefits to improving well-being, increasing engagement, and reducing burnout? And where should companies invest in order to improve the employee experience? An interesting report from PwC examined that exact question. It defined the employee experience as "the sum of all perceptions an employee has about the interactions with the organization in which he or she works" and explored 11 elements or drivers of a positive employee experience to see which, if any, impacted absenteeism, productivity, and turnover. The report found the following:[38]

1. A good employee experience leads to lower absenteeism, lower turnover, and higher productivity.
2. The 11 drivers that can impact employee experience include autonomy, development opportunities, reward, human-centered leadership, work environment, training, flexibility and schedule satisfaction, diversity, stress, well-being, and corporate social responsibility policies.

3. Well-being, providing development opportunities, and providing training for employees led to the best outcomes in
   terms of financial benefits to the company. The financial outcomes were expressed as a percentage of total turnover and
   investing in these three specifically showed savings of up
   to 4.9%.
4. Providing training to employees, decreasing workplace
   stress, focusing on developing human-centered leadership,
   and providing competitive compensation and benefits are
   the drivers most associated with reduced turnover.
5. Companies investing in all 11 drivers could realize a savings
   of up to 12.6% of total revenue.

Importantly, the report also found that investments in different elements of the employee experience had different effects,
which means that organizations need to take a variety of approaches
to make sure employees and teams continue to thrive. This is important because many organizations take a very general approach to
their well-being efforts. And most organizations get stuck here—at
the "beginner" stage—and make only a minor impact. Organizations
that become more proficient in this space, and thus see a more significant ROI associated with their efforts, take a more systemic
approach, which incorporates:

- Shared accountability for well-being among organizational
  leaders who prioritize it
- System-level interventions that are measured
- Consideration of well-being as a strategic investment
- A clearly articulated business case for well-being
- Operational decisions that consider well-being[39]

Marti Wronski helped me understand why leaders and
organizations can get stuck doing this work. Helping to identify and
unravel root causes or sources of stress, disconnection among teams,

silos, high workloads, and more can be grinding and painstaking work to do right and to do well. It takes time, involves lots of listening, and requires support from someone in the upper levels of the organization. In Marti's experience, leaders often drop off when they realize that there is so much to be fixed or unraveled and don't know where to start. When leaders find themselves in this situation, she said, they need to regroup and reground themselves in the *why* and consider whether a particular approach may not be working. Peeling back the organizational layers to get to the root causes is work, but it's work that's worth it.

Fortunately, there is now robust research to support your efforts. Happier workers are more productive, less likely to leave their jobs, less likely to miss days of work for health reasons, and tend to be more collaborative, creative, and committed to their jobs.[40] Researchers from Harvard and Oxford used crowd-sourced data from Indeed to examine the link between well-being and company performance. They looked at data from 1,636 publicly listed companies and measured employee well-being using the Indeed Work Well-Being Score, which looks at dimensions of work happiness, purpose, stress, and job satisfaction. They discovered that well-being was a significant predictor of company performance across a variety of indicators. Specifically, they found that higher levels of well-being generally predicted:

- Higher firm valuations
- Higher return on assets
- Higher gross profits
- Better stock market performance[41]

The researchers also found that higher levels of well-being are "not only predictive of contemporaneous company performance, but also of future firm performance."[42] This is so because they found that well-being positively influences productivity, creativity, social relationships, health, recruitment, and retention.[43]

Table 1.1. Comparing People + Performance Approaches

People + Performance-Focused (P+P-Focused): These companies outperformed on both financial results and human capital development. They represented 9% of the companies studied.	**People-Focused**: These companies outperformed on the human capital dimension. They represented 15% of the companies studied.
Performance-Focused: These companies outperformed on the financial results dimension. They represented 21% of the companies studied.	**Typical Performers**: These companies showed no distinct patterns and did not stand out in either dimension. They represented 55% of the companies studied.

Taking a People + Performance Approach Boosts the Bottom Line

Both Jen Fisher and Marti Wronski talked about how many leaders struggle to see that the people side of their leadership is as important as the performance side. Workload and general busyness, simply focusing more on the short-term business metrics and outcomes because that's what boards and CEOs demand, and/or legacy mindsets may all be reasons. Jen said that organizations must permit leaders to create a set of core competencies that allow them to develop as leaders but also to develop the skills to create an environment where people can flourish, and teams can take care of each other.

A McKinsey Global Institute report studying 1,793 large companies across multiple industry sectors in 15 countries found that companies that have a dual focus on developing human capital (defined in this report as the cumulative knowledge, skills, attributes, experience, and health of its workers) while also managing financial health have a performance edge. The report outlined four distinct categories, as shown in Table 1.1.[44]

The report found that the P+P-Focused companies:

- Were 4.3 times more likely than the average company to maintain top-tier financial performance for 9 out of 10 years from 2010 to 2019

- Grew their revenues two times faster than Performance-Focused companies from 2019 to 2021 (8% vs 4%)
- Had a lower attrition rate (8.5%) compared to the Performance-Focused companies (13.4%) and Typical Performers (13.5%), though slightly higher than the People-Focused companies (7.9%)
- Had returns on invested capital equal to the Performance-Focused companies (both 28%), but far better than the People-Focused companies (9%) and the Typical Performers (6%)
- Had greater economic profit ($1.1B) compared to the Performance-Focused companies ($0.4B)[45]

People-Focused companies and Typical Performers lagged behind both of the other categories as to financial results. The Performance-Focused companies remind me of many of the law firms and professional services firms generally with whom I have worked. They are very goal-oriented, top-down, and challenging environments, with a myopic focus on financial results. Many leaders in Performance-Focused companies have pressed me directly as to why they should change since clearly their model is making them money. As the report details, financial performance alone paints an incomplete picture. Performance-Focused companies experience more "bumps in the road" getting to the same destination compared to P+P-Focused companies. Specifically, "Where market trends are in their favor, these companies seem to be able to capture the upside well, but in periods of uncertainty, they lack the stability of the P+P-Focused companies. Not prioritizing human capital development seems to increase the exposure of performance-focused companies to volatility and risk in turbulent times."[46]

Organizations leave money on the table when they don't prioritize both human capital *and* financial performance. To help leaders find this balance and pursue healthy team cultures, we'll next explore the root causes of both stress and high performance.

Lead Well: Ideas to Remember

- The pandemic was an upheaval event that permanently changed how people think about work and how leaders need to think about leading.
- GenAI will require a new approach to leading—the future is humans + machines, not humans *or* machines.
- There is a gap between what employees prioritize and value at work and what leaders think they do. This gap needs to be addressed because leaders have an outsized role to play in their teams' well-being.
- Companies need to create and invest in long-term strategies for developing healthy, thriving teams, much like they already do in the areas of finance, operations, and technology.
- There is a strong business case supporting the creation of positive cultures. Leaders need to recognize the financial and performance benefits associated with creating healthy teams.

Chapter 2

Why Work Isn't Working

Examining the root causes of chronic stress is an important step for organizations. Formally assessing sources of stress often confirms known issues but can sometimes reveal surprises. A large professional services firm specializing in architecture and interior design approached me to help them better understand sources of team stress and burnout, and they were keen from the very start to focus on root causes. We invited 32 leaders on their senior management team to take an assessment to help better understand the deeper issues at play.

From the start, the team knew that workload was a problem. Our assessment showed that this was the leading issue, and the CEO was not at all surprised by this finding. But what *was* surprising was that I also discovered that many of the senior leaders answered questions about cultural fairness with "hard to decide." That puzzled me since they dictated the culture, so I raised the issue with the CEO.

The CEO and her team had been consciously trying to dismantle perceptions of cultural unfairness in a variety of ways. In fact, the CEO had ascended to her position as part of management changes meant to address these concerns. They were frustrated to learn that their efforts had stalled, at least among the senior leadership team. While I knew she was discouraged, I pointed out that this information could help her kick-start important conversations about how to pivot their efforts. I will tell you more about the initial steps the team took to address the workload issue in chapter 5.

Digging into the true causes of why your team is stressed, dismantling silos at work, and figuring out how to better engage your people takes time. While I hope that you will see that the Lead Well mindsets are easy to implement, I don't want to oversimplify the amount of work it takes over the long term to create a workplace that truly works. That's why some of my favorite work involves helping organizations begin this process.

In addition, the Lead Well mindsets will help organizations take a more balanced "me and we" approach to their well-being and workplace culture conversations.

Working Well Requires Taking a "Me and a We" Approach

When asked specifically about what undermines their health at work, employees frequently cite workplace environment factors like always being on call, unmanageable workloads, low autonomy, and lack of social support.[47] If employers stay focused on the "me" or individual side of this equation without addressing the "we" side, then they may see weaker improvements in employee mental health and engagement given their investment. Individual-focused skills alone can't compensate for unsupportive workplace factors.

Focusing on the "we" side of the equation involves two parts. It means (1) addressing the workplace root causes or sources of chronic stress and disengagement *and* (2) educating leaders about how to create positive team cultures that are promotive of thriving. It's important that organizations take a balanced approach that prioritizes short-term ideas with long-term strategies to create the positive cultures employees seek.[48]

Part 1: Address the Root Causes of Chronic Stress & Disengagement

Research has consistently identified six main drivers of chronic stress and disengagement at work, which serve as a useful starting point for leaders.[49] I call them the "Core 6." Table 2.1 describes their characteristics.

The Core 6 framework is an easy way to begin evaluating individual and team stressors using the "we" lens. The leaders with whom I've worked have helped me see both the nuance and interconnectivity in the Core 6 framework.

First, there is a lot of subjectivity in this framework. What is an unmanageable workload for me might look very different for you. In addition, there is fluidity. What is an unmanageable workload at

Table 2.1. Core 6 Drivers of Chronic Stress & Disengagement

Core 6 Driver	Characteristics
Unmanageable workload	You consistently have too much to do, and you feel like you're treading water and at any moment you might sink. Unmanageable workload leads to more unhealthy forms of stress than does high workload. High workload, while stressful, acts as a motivational booster. Unmanageable workload does the opposite. **Note**: One of my workshop attendees asked about having too little work. While it's not as prominently featured in the research, having a consistently low or unpredictable workload can also be stressful.
Lack of recognition	You don't hear a lot of positive feedback, and you're not often thanked for your efforts. You may feel excluded from important meetings, projects, deals, visible work, and other important events when you perceive that has been earned. You may get frustrated when you are working at a certain level and your title doesn't match your perceived effort.
Lack of community and connection	You don't feel part of a cohesive team, you don't feel like your leader has your back or otherwise supports your work, you don't have supportive and trustworthy colleagues, and you don't report having a close friend at work.
Unfairness	You notice favoritism—it's not what you do, it's who you know—that dictates how you advance in your career. You must consistently navigate organizational politics and red tape. You notice a lot of "closed door" meetings with little clarity or transparency as to direction and decisions that will impact your work.
Values misalignment	Your personal values about work and what you want from your work experience don't match your organization's values. This is an increasing area of stress on work teams as different cohorts of workers approach work with different values.
Lack of autonomy/ control/flexibility	You want the freedom to be able to do your work free from micromanagement, poor leadership, and ineffective teaming practices. You want a say in how you achieve your goals and the route you take to accomplish tasks and projects.

age 25 might look different at 45 when you are raising a family and/ or caring for elderly parents or relatives. These factors alone make one-size-fits-all approaches in this space difficult.

Second, the items on this list are interconnected. Most, if not all, of the teams I talk to have an unmanageable workload issue that is, in many instances, getting worse. Being too busy impacts all the other factors listed on this chart. If you're too busy and barely keeping your head above water, the odds that you will notice something great that your direct report did and thus recognize him or her for it in the moment is low. Increased pressure to perform or make your numbers might lead to micromanaging projects because you lack the confidence in your team, thus undercutting autonomy. Unfairness eats away at the fabric of having a cohesive team and psychologically safe environment in which to work.

Finally, the owner of a landscape company who attended one of my workshops suggested that a good approach would be to start by improving one of the Core 6. That improvement would then have positive ripple effects with the other factors on that list. He decided to start with lack of recognition, but I've had other leaders advocate just as strongly for starting with community. Or values misalignment. Wherever you start, the process is essentially the same: intentionally addressing one root cause at a time to start noticing positive systemic outcomes.

I always ask participants to spend time talking about the Core 6 in my workshops. It's usually the first time they have associated the Core 6 with their own or their teams' experience of stress and disengagement, and the framework helps them to more fully explain and understand why they feel stressed and burned out. There are always wonderful questions and observations that come from these discussions. Here are common themes I hear (in their words):

- It would be nice if we could have more fun at work. Fun builds community.
- On paper, my workload might be manageable, but it's been so consistently high for so long, and that takes a toll.

- Our workload is high because we don't have the budget to hire more people; there is economic uncertainty and talk of layoffs, so nobody wants to say "no."
- What does community at work even mean *today*? This needs to be better defined and more intentional. The office is one of many tools now to accomplish work.
- Unmanageable workloads get labeled/disguised as "productivity" and it's financially rewarded.
- Work is getting more complex, but teams aren't getting bigger.
- Recognition doesn't always feel authentic because senior leadership doesn't really understand or know what our team does. We need a team PR person.
- How do I say no and establish boundaries without feeling guilty? Or fearing repercussions? Leaders need to provide "cover."
- It's stressful not knowing which way to go and who to go to, and how to get what you need to be successful.
- Sometimes unmanageable workload looks like a combination of high workload at work and high workload at home. How do you address this type of unmanageable workload?

This is only a small sampling of what we discuss. You can see that people have a lot of questions and insights in this area. I strongly encourage everyone in my workshops to screenshot or otherwise capture the Core 6 framework, make it consistently visible to the team, and continue to discuss it after I finish my work.

A school superintendent in one of my workshops raised a great point. He wondered whether his people might have been speaking in Core 6 language about their stressors all along, and since he didn't know the framework, he didn't "hear" their words. Now he could more consciously listen for Core 6 themes. The framework is a vital starting point and provides common language for teams to talk about the root causes of chronic stress and disengagement.

Part 2: Leverage the Root Amplifiers of Thriving

Traditionally, organizations have focused on developing an employee's functional or technical skills. As work becomes more uncertain and less predictable, people must be motivated to adapt to changing conditions and to try new ways of working. In addition, leaders need to understand the core drivers and workplace experiences that form the psychology of motivation and high performance. Just like the Core 6 help leaders and teams uncover the key drivers and root causes of burnout and disengagement, the ABCs help leaders and teams unlock the positive opposite: thriving.

What Are the ABCs?

There are three essential nutrients at the heart of thriving, intrinsic motivation, engagement, and high performance at work:[50]

- **Autonomy (control and choice)**: You feel like you have some choice as to how and when you perform the various tasks that make up your job and in how you execute your daily responsibilities; you have a say in the way things are done; and you can take initiative and make decisions about your work. Autonomy does not mean going it alone or individualism.
- **Belonging (connection)**: You feel connected to your colleagues; you feel like you belong to groups that are important and significant to you; you feel cared for by others; and you value creating high-quality relationships and friendships at work.
- **Challenge (growth)**: You feel like you're getting better at goals that matter to you; you feel effective in your work role; and you want to continue to grow and develop as a professional and master new skills.[51]

I will refer to these essential nutrients throughout this book as "the ABCs" or "ABC needs." I wrote about the ABCs in my first book.

At that time, I identified this trio as an important part of the "anti-burnout" team environment, and their importance has only increased in the workplace well-being and performance conversation. In fact, the ABCs are a foundational aspect of two large-scale, national well-being frameworks: the US Surgeon General's Framework for Workplace Mental Health & Well-Being[52] and the National Academy of Medicine's *Taking Action Against Clinician Burnout: A Systems Approach to Professional Well-Being.*[53]

In addition, unmet ABC needs are a significant part of disengagement at work. Organizations can save up to $56 million of the total $90 million at stake from disengagement at work by focusing on these six employee factors:[54]

1. Inadequate total compensation
2. Lack of meaningful work
3. Lack of workplace flexibility **(A—Autonomy)**
4. Lack of career development and enhancement **(C—Challenge)**
5. Unreliable and unsupportive people at work **(B—Belonging)**
6. Unsafe workplace environment

These factors also map onto or could be subcategories of the Core 6. As you can see, unmet ABC needs are three out of six drivers of disengagement. Companies are losing millions of dollars by not prioritizing these needs.

Further, research reveals that there are six leadership practices that foster meaningful work:[55]

1. Communicate the work's bigger impact
2. Recognize and nurture potential **(C—Challenge)**
3. Foster personal connections **(B—Belonging)**
4. Discuss values and purpose during hiring
5. Lead in alignment with stated organizational values
6. Give employees freedom **(A—Autonomy)**

Meeting ABC needs forms a substantial part of the leadership practices that foster meaningful work, and I'll explore these practices in more detail in chapter 7.

Finally, ABC needs form the basis for specific job resources that help drive thriving at work. Job resources are aspects of work that help employees meet and manage the stress caused by the different job demands they experience, enable the achievement of goals, and promote learning and growth.[56] New research suggests that while many different job resources influence work engagement, three are critical to activating it:[57]

1. Skill discretion: being able to use different skills, be creative, and learn new things at work. (**A—Autonomy**)
2. Feedback: seeing the results of your accomplishments and understanding how your work fits within the group context. (**B—Belonging & C—Challenge**)
3. Team empowerment, which includes the following four components: (**all ABC needs**)
   a. Team efficacy (a team's belief in its ability to cope with a broad range of stressful or challenging demands and to succeed);
   b. Meaningfulness (your work has meaning and leaders know the specific practices that foster meaningful work);
   c. Autonomy (you have some freedom and flexibility); and
   d. Impact (you know your work matters).

Leading in a way that promotes and emphasizes these and other resources is connected to increased work engagement and lower burnout.[58] Overall, while the ABCs form the basis for thriving and high performance at work, you can see that they unlock much more than that. The ABCs play a very important role in influencing your overall well-being, promoting engagement, amplifying meaningful work, and mitigating the stress associated with job demands.

I love the creative ways the teams with whom I have worked have incorporated ABC concepts into their daily work. Some teams have included ABC principles and targeted questions into their review processes. Others have embedded ABC ideas into onboarding training and in their mentoring programs. You'll learn more about ABC needs in chapter 4.

A Disjointed Approach to Employee Thriving: The Silos That Interfere

The speaking inquiries I receive come from a variety of departments and from people with a variety of titles. I may be asked to position my work as "leadership and teaming," or as well-being, stress management, resilience, or something similar. I wasn't tracking that this might lead to a disjointed approach and thus influence the efficacy and impact of my work. That changed when a student in a certificate course I co-teach asked, "You are talking about the overlap of burnout and engagement and burnout and depression, and these topics intersect. But on a practical level, these topics are often siloed off within different groups that have different responsibilities (and different budgets). There needs to be a more holistic view of these topics, but what do we do when the teams responsible for these topics are in their own silos?"

His question led me to think more deeply about the silos that exist in the context of training and programming this work:[59]

- **HR benefits/wellness/well-being:** These are professionals who are tasked with administering employee assistance programs, health plans, and tending to the basic well-being needs of employees.
- **HR learning & development/educational development/ talent development:** These are professionals who are responsible for employee education and training, upskilling, and professional growth (in the service of performance and productivity).
- **Diversity, equity, & inclusion:** These are professionals who are responsible for ensuring people of various backgrounds

feel welcome and have the support they need to perform to the fullest of their abilities at work.

- **Employee engagement:** I see these teams and titles showing up more in the legal profession as it discovers this area of work. These are professionals who are responsible for assessing the strength of the connection employees feel toward their work and organizations. Other industries may house these professionals in their HR departments or may see "building engagement" as part of the HR function without the need to have people be given such titles explicitly.

The problem with these silos is that in a changing and uncertain future of work, workers' well-being and professional development needs will continue to intersect. In an uncertain environment, the skills that you need to manage stress are the same ones that activate career growth and learning.[60] You can't beat burnout until you deal with the "we" side—cultural leader-centric factors that create stress and challenge in the first place. As with the conversation about GenAI, leaders need to identify the skills that will mitigate uncertainty and train people in those skills now as new technologies develop.

"It Takes Time," "Not My Responsibility," & "How Do We Measure?"

Let's be honest. Not all leaders think it's part of their job to foster a positive team culture. Many corporate leaders take too much of a short-term approach to engagement and well-being, stalling most efforts before they can get started. Marti Wronski is not one of those people. You met Marti, the chief operating officer of the Milwaukee Brewers, in chapter 1. Her long-term goal is to create a best-in-class culture. In pursuing that, it didn't take her long to realize that she needed to address the silos that existed in the organization. Silos cause problems in two ways: by making the programming and training of this work difficult and then impeding cross-collaboration within internal teams as to the function and execution of the actual work.[61]

To get the teams to work more cross-collaboratively, she started by meeting with each team individually: PR, sales, communications, marketing, and box office. She then blocked time for the team leads to meet together and purchased three wall calendars: one for last year, one for this year, and one for next year. Each team lead wrote their programs, ideas, projects, and initiatives, month by month, year by year, until all the information was captured and color-coded by team. At the end of the exercise, she said, jaws dropped. They realized they had very little insight into each other's work.

Once the teams clearly saw each other's work, they could then create one cohesive strategy, with each team owning their part. And while Marti took on this work herself, she told me that she created a new role (which has become a new department, Business Analytics) that has helped her tremendously by measuring ROI outcomes and identifying problem areas. There can be considerable challenge in proving ROI in this space, and chief financial officers speak the language of efficiency.

These are some other ideas organizations may wish to consider:

1. **Develop and deliver programming and resources in different formats.** Teams need to take a variety of approaches to engage employees and promote thriving.[62] For example, leaders can consider live or virtual workshops, a virtual program series, on-demand content in the form of short videos, 1:1 coaching, and printed resources like summary charts and worksheets.

2. **Break down the silos with close, frequent collaboration and communication.** Leaders in each vertical need to work together to strategically plan how to take a holistic view of well-being, leadership needs, and the actual execution of the work (front-line employees have different needs than managers, who have different needs than leaders). The larger the company, the harder it may be to really know who your peers

are across these silos and/or to easily cross-collaborate with other teams. Here are some useful steps to follow:

- Start by listing the key stakeholders in each department and your peers on each team. You may have to make a few calls or peruse your company's intranet to get started.
- Then list the types of programs each vertical produces and curates.
- Note the overlaps. How can you collaborate on programs? How can you share budgets?
- Know your audience. How can you market these programs to use language that emphasizes well-being and performance components as applicable? For example, if you want to talk to C-level leaders about burnout, you should emphasize the Core 6, the business case, and the role that leaders play in the prevention of burnout.

3. **Hire for behavioral sciences fluency on your teams, particularly someone who is well-versed on the prevention side of the well-being equation.** I work with smart people, but part of the reason they seek me out is that they lack this expertise. Even if the silos get dismantled, professionals may still find themselves stuck trying to tease apart the nuances of these topics, and they may lack the expertise to determine what offerings will move the needle.

Taking a root-cause approach to both the problem and the solution is important. The individual tactics that were such a part of the pandemic response to stress will have more of their intended impact once upstream solutions are also created. And while the Milwaukee Brewers are still in the early stages of their efforts, Marti has reported that team creativity is "off the charts," and people are happier. People are oriented now around a common goal and a cohesive strategy across departments. She notices people cross-collaborating and "riffing" off each other to create innovative ideas. Importantly, since team leaders have clearly identified goals, they can better direct their teams. And they can explicitly outline the impact each person has on the team, which makes everyone feel appreciated. Further, starting to measure outcomes has helped remove blame and finger-pointing when issues arise.

The Lead Well mindsets in the next five chapters will help you address the institutional problems created by the Core 6—and the future of work factors I shared in the introduction—and give you the skills you need to build the ABC needs and other capacities that will be required to create positive team cultures now and in an uncertain future.

Lead Well: Ideas to Remember

- Your teams won't reach their full performance potential until you uncover and address the root sources of chronic stress and disengagement and address them, before actively seeking to incorporate the root drivers of thriving and high performance.
- There are six root causes of disengagement and chronic stress (the Core 6) and three root drivers of thriving and high performance (the ABCs).
- The Core 6 help you identify starting points to address chronic stress on your team. They are interconnected, and it often helps to start with one.
- The ABCs play a very important role in influencing your overall well-being, promoting engagement, amplifying meaningful work, and mitigating the stress associated with job demands.
- Workplace silos can stall your efforts to both teach and train these concepts, and to help your teams work cross-collaboratively.

PART II

The Lead Well Mindsets

Chapter 3

Mindset #1
Prioritize Sticky Recognition & Mattering

M ost people don't attend Ivy League universities for the dust-free desks and the yummy meals. Support staff at universities and most workplaces often go unnoticed, but Rahan Staton is on a mission to change that.[63] Rahan is a recent graduate of Harvard Law School, but before attending there, he worked at a sanitation and trash removal company refurbishing dumpsters. While doing that work, he said, "people would point to me and my coworker and literally say, 'Don't be like them.'" So, when he got to Harvard, Rahan made it his mission to make sure the support staff felt recognized and seen. Known for his heartfelt hugs to the custodians and cafeteria workers, Rahan wanted to do more than say some kind words. So, he created a nonprofit called the Reciprocity Effect, whose mission is to make sure that support staff, at Harvard and beyond, feel recognized and valued. How can such simple gestures transform entire cultures?

There are six aspects of work that are critically important to employees that leaders consistently overlook (and underemphasize): being valued by my manager; being valued by my organization; having caring and trusting teammates; potential for advancement; a sense of belonging; and flexible work schedules.[64] The first two—being valued by my manager and being valued by my organization—are the subject of this chapter, and it's typically where I suggest leaders start within the Lead Well framework.

There is an organization that has built its entire culture around the importance of making sure its employees feel recognized and valued—Lifepoint Health (Lifepoint). Lifepoint is a diversified health-care delivery network consisting of community hospitals, rehabilitation and behavioral health hospitals, and additional sites of care across the United States. It has more than 55,000 employees and operates across 30 states. I interviewed Jason Zachariah, Lifepoint's executive vice president and chief operating officer, to learn more about how Lifepoint embeds recognition into the fabric of its business, and in doing so, nurtures some of the most caring and engaged employees I have encountered.[65]

Lifepoint created a culture of recognition by focusing on its mission, vision, and values as the starting point.[66] Lifepoint's core values are: Champion Patient Care; Do the Right Thing; Embrace Individuality; Act with Kindness; and Make a Difference Together. Jason said leaders are expected to adopt the core values and espouse them in their thoughts, words, and deeds. They are expected to appear in company initiatives as well. He noted that they hardwired the values into a recognition platform called "Making Moments Matter." Making Moments Matter is a digital platform that individuals, their peer groups, manager, and manager's manager can all see. The company has more than 300,000 recognitions since launching the platform in 2023.

While Lifepoint is an exemplar in this category, in our lengthy workshop discussions, most leaders admitted that recognition wasn't something that they did well (or at all). Even if their teams or organizations did have some type of recognition or appreciation program, it was just that: a codified day to say thanks or a recognition check-in based on years of service. It was helpful, but nothing personal or specific. When recognition sticks, important business and well-being outcomes follow. Yet, many managers are unsure about how to make their team members feel like their contributions are noticed and valued.

Being slow to recognize has consequences. Respondents to a recent Deloitte workplace well-being survey cited lack of recognition as one of the three most detrimental leadership behaviors to their well-being.[67] In a survey study I conducted with American Law

Media, many of the nearly 900 lawyers and legal professionals who responded said lack of recognition was a source of stress, with 44.1% saying they were recognized only once a month, a few times a year or less, or never.[68]

There are lots of different ways to recognize people at work.[69] Formal recognition tends to be described as company-wide awards, often given annually. Informal recognition can be anything from celebrating birthdays and retirements to acknowledging when a team finishes an important project. Everyday recognition is the regular sharing of thanks and positive feedback to all levels of employees.

The type of recognition I'm focused on is the type that causes people to remember the act or the words months or even years later. It's something I call "sticky" recognition, which I define as recognition that shows people and teams the evidence of their impact. Gold watches and gift cards are nice, but they aren't sticky. In addition, because many companies aren't strategically focused on recognition, they tend to focus more heavily on recognition *programs* and neglect the need for recognition *practices*.[70] Lifepoint does both.

In addition to the Making Moments Matter platform, Lifepoint also honors one of its employees with its Mercy Award each year. The award is named after Lifepoint's founding chairman and CEO, Scott Mercy, and it's the highest honor a Lifepoint employee can receive. I had the privilege of speaking at the Mercy Awards event in 2023 about the importance of human-centered leadership. As part of my preparation to speak, I received a booklet with the stories of the nominees, including the winner. After reading more than 100 biographies, I was so inspired to improve my own recognition and kindness practices.

Everyday Sticky Recognition: Start with a Thank You "Plus"

While not every company can hold a big annual event, the act of creating moments of sticky recognition starts with a sentence or two and a few minutes of your time. Here is an example of what sticky recognition sounds like. It's what I call a thank you "plus." When you say thank you, add a couple of additional sentences that describe the strengths or behaviors that you saw that generated the good outcome. Even though it's only a sentence or two, phrasing it this way more clearly shows a person the evidence of their impact.

I found this short vignette on LinkedIn, and it was written by a former practicing lawyer. It illustrates the brevity and power of a thank you "plus." She writes:

> When I was a junior associate, I had a tedious assignment to summarize a set of deposition transcripts for a partner. It wasn't glamourous or exciting, but I did it, sent it in, and moved on. Three weeks later, I saw the partner's name pop up on my caller ID. My first reaction was an inner groan, because I wasn't clamoring to comb through another set of deposition transcripts, but I picked up anyway. To my great surprise, the partner told me that he was just calling to say thanks. "I know that probably wasn't the most exciting project you've had, *but the summaries were clearly organized and helped me find the key takeaways quickly. Just wanted to say thanks.*" The whole conversation lasted maybe 120 seconds, but I still remember it almost 14 years later. And going forward, I said yes to any assignment he called with—and that's how I got my first federal court argument.[71]

I put the sticky part in italics. The first thing the partner did is that he noticed her work and her effort. Then he told her about its impact in a very specific way. When you receive recognition that is sticky, it's hard to forget. And notice how she said that his efforts caused her to say "yes to any assignment he called with." Researchers have found that people who express appreciation are seen as warmer and more competent and caring about others, and the people being thanked do extra work for them.[72]

Sticky Recognition Leads to Mattering

When I read the short vignette above, and then reflected on the all-too-infrequent instances of sticky recognition I've received in my work life, I wondered: Why does this specific type of recognition stick so much? Why does it cause you to build strong trust with someone, remember conversations, and keep notes years and years later? The answer is that it activates mattering, which is a fundamental human need.

Mattering is defined as your sense of the difference you make in the world.[73] It's about significance, and it's composed of two parts. The first part of mattering is that you feel valued (appreciation and recognition) and the second part is that you know you're adding value (achievement).[74] You feel important, noticed, and needed.[75] The pandemic was an upheaval event that amplified our search for meaning and purpose. It revealed a great deal about what people had been experiencing in their work and their lives. It revealed that people felt invisible, unseen, and unheard. And the social isolation many experienced only served to amplify what was already going on pre-pandemic. We started to think more deeply about our own significance, and whether we felt seen in our communities, in our families, and at work.

Mattering unlocks a potent mix of psychological and motivational fuel. When employees feel like they matter to their organization, they are more satisfied with their jobs and life, are more likely to seek out leadership positions, are less likely to quit, and have lower rates of burnout, depression, and anxiety.[76] In addition, they report higher relationship satisfaction and more self-compassion, and they have a greater belief in their ability to achieve their goals.[77]

Mattering is also an indicator of organizational health and employee success. Mattering at work is significantly associated with work meaning, job satisfaction, and commitment to the organization.[78] Feeling valued at work is also related to lower absenteeism, better employee-manager relationships, greater resilience, less job stress, and increased well-being.[79]

One study asked this simple question to nearly 2,000 people: "What do you feel your employer values most about you?"[80] They responded in a variety of ways, and their responses were categorized into three different groups as follows:

- **Group 1:** Those who answered the question with statements like, "My overall talent and skill" and "My inherent worth as a human being."
- **Group 2:** Those who answered the question with statements like, "My productivity" and "My responsiveness and availability."
- **Group 3:** Those who answered the question with statements like, "I don't know—I get very little feedback" and "Not much—my employer does not make me feel valued."

People were then asked to answer questions about their levels of perceived stress, mental and physical health, and work over-commitment. The results showed a clear health hierarchy. The people in Group 1 reported much better mental health, followed by Group 2, and then Group 3. In addition, people in Groups 2 and 3 were much more likely to answer "yes" to the question "Are you considering leaving, or have you left your profession due to mental health, burnout, or stress?" with 26.7% of Group 2 and 37.4% of Group 3 saying "yes," compared to 15.4% of the people in Group 1.

Recognition Roadblocks

If creating a culture of sticky recognition and mattering is easy (you can literally do it right now), doesn't take much time (a couple of min-utes or less in most cases), and is free, why don't we do it? Adrian, a senior leader at a chemical distribution company, voiced it this way: "Where's the line between recognition and someone just doing their job? I can't always be recognizing people." His question stirred up a lot of conversation, and in this workshop and others, leaders revealed a lot of their deeper feelings about appreciation and recognition and why they don't necessarily prioritize something that is so easy. Here are some of their remarks:

- I'm too busy—I'm supposed to add *this* to my list of things to do now?
- I'm too focused on preventing mistakes that I forget to mention or don't amplify what's right.
- It's not urgent—I don't think that someone will walk out the door tomorrow because I didn't thank them today.
- It's not my job to be your cheerleader.
- You get a paycheck—that's thanks enough.
- It feels like "everyone gets a trophy" mentality.

I talked to Dr. Zachary Mercurio, a prominent researcher in the science of mattering, and he said that adults need to have a secure base from which to venture out, explore, and connect.[81] Mattering helps people feel psychologically nourished in the same way that food helps us feel physically full. Without that nourishment, workers will start to feel psychologically "hangry," and the result is quiet quitting, conduct issues, blaming, and gossip. This is the language of the unheard and unseen according to Zach.

Separately, recognition isn't about stroking someone's ego. It's about giving the people who you value the psychological fuel to feel engaged. When leaders don't take the opportunity to appreciate their teams, there are consequences. The people who you value may end up feeling like just a cog in the work wheel, and that's the opposite of mattering. In my survey study with American Law Media, I wanted to know how many people felt this way. What I found was that 51.4% of the respondents said, "I feel like a cog in the wheel at work" once a week or more. More worrisome, 23.1% said they felt that way every day.[82] People devote a huge percentage of their lives to work. A little thanks goes a long way.

Skills That Build Sticky Recognition & Mattering

In addition to the thank you "plus" skill I mentioned above, there are other simple ways to increase sticky recognition and mattering on your teams. Here are a few TNTs for you to try.

TNT: ACKNOWLEDGE OTHERS

Zach said that, at its essence, building a culture of mattering is done by just being human. First, he suggested, leaders need to build the skills to *see* people—you must learn, or relearn, how to pay attention to another person. The number-one thing you can do to increase mattering is to simply acknowledge people. Miss them when they are gone. Tell them how you rely on them. He said that simply spending time with people and seeing them is the "currency" of mattering. And, mattering lives in the in-between moments of your day-to-day interactions. What do you say to people in the 10 minutes before the meeting starts? When you're walking down the hall together?

TNT: NOTICE & NAME STRENGTHS

Another way to increase mattering is to know and regularly name people's unique strengths, perspectives, and their vision. I was out to dinner with a good friend of mine recently. As we were leaving the restaurant, he hopped into the car as I bumped into a friend who was just going inside to eat. I hadn't seen her in a few years and gave her the biggest hug. When I got in the car, my friend said, "I love how your face lights up when you see your friends." It was more than a compliment. He noticed something about me that *I* value—my kindness (and the importance of my friends)—and told me about it. I'll never forget how it made me feel.

TNT: MORE STICKY RECOGNITION & MATTERING BUILDERS

Here are some additional ideas to help you build sticky recognition and mattering, many of which also work at home and within your broader communities:

- Share your belief in someone and their capabilities.
- Let someone know how you rely on them.
- Talk as a team (or a family) about lessons learned when failure and challenge happen.
- Acknowledge the effort a person put forth.
- Invest time with someone.
- Remember someone's name.
- Say "Good morning!" Employees report that simply hearing "good morning" from a manager can be as meaningful as formal recognition.[83]
- Discuss growth potential and give people stretch assignments (both are indicators of value).[84]

I asked Jason Zachariah at Lifepoint what he would say to leaders who think, "This is too soft," or "It's not my job to recognize people at work." He was clear, and his argument starts with talent attraction and retention. He sees recognition as an integral way for his organization, and organizations in any industry, to meet capacity needs. When a leader says they can't retain personnel, and they explain the reasons for that based on macro workplace trends or business economics, he views that as a convenience argument. It's hard work, and it takes intentionality and practice to live your company values and recognize people in accordance with those values.

Younger generations are looking for work environments that give them a sense of nurturing, safety, signals that leaders care about them, kindness, and the ability to see a long-term future at the organization. Jason was extremely intentional about building a cadre of leaders around him who could authentically act in this way because he views this mindset as the company's biggest controllable tool for retention and recruitment. And carrying that one step further, he believes that if they can attract the best talent, a great employee experience will translate into a great patient experience.

One of the food service cashiers who met Rahan Staton said this of his efforts: "You don't even realize how unseen you were until you were seen. And once you are, you realize, this is kind of nice." Writing this chapter has changed how I look at my own relationships. I now try to bring an intentionality of mattering to my interactions with my daughter, Lucy, with my friends, and with my loved ones in a way I don't think I have before. Rahan, Jason, Zach and others have helped me slow down and appreciate the gift we all have in being with and simply acknowledging one another.

Lead Well: Ideas to Remember

- One of the easiest and quickest ways to address chronic stress and disengagement at work is with sticky recognition.
- Sticky recognition leads to mattering. There are important business and well-being outcomes that occur when a person feels like they matter at work.
- Mattering has two parts—you know you're adding value (achievement) and you feel valued (recognition). You also feel noticed, important, and needed.
- Saying a thank you "plus" is one of the best ways to convey sticky recognition.
- There are also many TNTs that help activate both sticky recognition and mattering. Pick one or two and practice consistently.
- Review the roadblocks list and reflect on whether you need to reframe how you think about recognition.

Chapter 4

Mindset #2
Amplify ABC Needs

A BC needs (autonomy, belonging, and challenge) are at the heart of employee motivation, engagement, and high performance.[85]

One organization that has found a way to amplify ABC needs in a unique way is Sidley Austin, LLP (Sidley). Sidley is a large law firm headquartered in the United States with more than 20 offices around the globe. I interviewed Yvette Ostolaza, Sidley's Management Committee chair and Executive Committee member, because I heard about an innovative leadership development program Sidley created for its associates.[86] It caught my attention because, as a former practicing lawyer, I know that leadership development is a topic that is often underprioritized in the legal profession.

The idea for this program originated when Yvette attended a course at Harvard about workplace disruption. As part of the course, she was asked the question, "What jobs might need to be fixed either at your firm or in your industry?" As she considered her answer, she knew she wanted to create something that not only focused on leadership training, but also helped people reconnect post-pandemic. Thanks to her vision, Sidley launched Built to Lead®, a professional development initiative designed to enhance associates' leadership skills, business acumen, and connection with each other.

Sidley partnered with the external executive education programs at Northwestern's Kellogg School of Management and Columbia Business School to create a stackable program that starts in a lawyer's fourth year of practice. Associates complete a weeklong external executive education program at either Northwestern or Columbia, where participants earn a certificate from the business school they attended. In addition, lawyers are promoted to Managing Associate, reflecting their increasing responsibility for leading teams (autonomy). Critically, Yvette also wants clients to recognize the inflection points in their attorneys' careers.

In year five, lawyers complete an internal executive leadership academy and gain access to individual career coaching with an external coach (challenge and growth). In year six, associates spend time together completing service projects with select nonprofit legal and community organizations, along with civic leadership training (belonging and connection). Associates are again promoted in year seven to Senior Managing Associate and complete an internal executive leadership academy focused on skills needed to credibly counsel boards and senior executives. Business development coaching, focused on building and solidifying the skills and relationships that are key to creating a sustainable legal career, follows in year eight.

In addition, Sidley's partners also expressed a strong interest in further developing their leadership and business skills. So, in 2024, Sidley launched Built to Lead 2.0, an executive leadership program for firm partners and clients, providing partners with additional opportunities to connect and collaborate with each other and with clients.

I defined the ABC needs in chapter 2, illustrating that they play a powerful psychological role in influencing your overall well-being, promoting engagement, amplifying meaningful work, and mitigating the stress of job demands by promoting thriving and higher performance.

Leaders can enhance their team's ABC needs in both big and small ways. Let's now take a closer look at each of the ABC needs, and, importantly, how they can be developed in a distributed workplace.

Autonomy: The Need to "Choose Your Own Adventure"

When you were growing up, did you read any of the books in the Choose Your Own Adventure series? Page by page, you got to decide what the characters did or didn't do, ultimately informing how the story ended. Another way to think about autonomy is the fundamental need to "choose your own adventure," both in life and in work. Employees at all levels want the ability to decide for themselves how their work story will unfold, day-to-day, week-to-week, and over the long haul. Autonomy is linked to work engagement, lower rates of burnout, intrinsic motivation, and seeing one's work as meaningful.[87]

Autonomy challenges can appear in different ways for leaders. A woman named Raquel approached me after a recent workshop. She told me about her new role as a senior leader in a chemical distribution company. We had talked about the Core 6 as part of my workshop, and she zeroed in on the autonomy segment. She explained that she was having a tough time figuring out how much latitude to provide each of her direct reports. Some wanted a bit more hand-holding, more than she found she had time for, while others felt better with minimal interaction.

Separately, a sales executive and I were talking in the lunch line after one of my workshops, and he said that he and his team had previously enjoyed maximum autonomy in their work. He could directly sign off on projects and resources, and he enjoyed that. But when his small company was eventually acquired by a larger organization, the culture immediately changed. Not only did he and his team lose a lot of autonomy, but that loss also created a sense of unfairness in the form of more organizational politics and red tape, which slowed down his team and created an "us versus them" mentality between existing and new employees (remember that the Core 6 components influence each other).

As a leader, you may need to dial up or dial back how involved you are given your team's autonomy needs. You may also need to rethink what autonomy looks like.

Broaden Your Thinking about Autonomy

What I often find is that the conversation about workplace flexibility has become too narrow in that it's usually focused solely on where and when people work. If you think about autonomy more broadly in terms of helping those on your team chose their own adventure, then you open other avenues for building autonomy that you might not have expected. Autonomy is about freedom and choice. Table 4.1 shows different types of autonomy at work for you to consider incorporating with your team.

Time to Reflect

Where are you able to help influence your employees' autonomy needs? Company policy may prevent you from giving them the

Table 4.1. Different Autonomy Types

Autonomy Type	Definition
Schedule autonomy	Team members have the freedom to choose when and where they work.
Task autonomy	The degree of independence team members have in deciding how to perform their job tasks and assignments. You may provide a high-level overview of goals and strategy, and they decide how to get from Point A to Point B.
Decision-making autonomy	The authority team members have in making decisions related to their work, such as setting priorities, allocating resources, and solving problems. You are empowered to exercise judgment and discretion in determining the best course of action to take to achieve goals and objectives. See the TNTs below for a specific exercise.
Creative autonomy	Teams can explore new ideas, experiment with different approaches, and they are encouraged to innovate and take risks.
Career autonomy	You can set career goals, pursue learning opportunities, and make decisions about career path and skill development opportunities.
Social autonomy	Your team can choose how to communicate, collaborate, and build relationships with colleagues, clients, and stakeholders.

flexibility to be fully remote, but can you give them more decision-making autonomy or task autonomy? Better yet, show them Table 4.1 and ask for their input. Also consider that a person's autonomy needs may change over time.

Take the Quiz

If you're curious about whether your team members have enough autonomy, ask them to take this quiz by answering each statement with a "yes" or "no".[88]

1. I feel like I have some choice in how I execute my day-to-day responsibilities.
2. I have a say in the way my day-to-day work gets done.
3. I am part of the decision-making process on changes that impact me and my work.
4. I have the necessary skills *and* support to improve my day-to-day work.
5. I have the necessary resources to do my job effectively.
6. I am encouraged to provide new and innovative solutions to challenges.
7. I have control over my career development in this organization.
8. I can choose how I want to build relationships with others on my team and within the organization.

Discuss any "no" responses as a team, then use Table 4.1 to discuss ideas and goals for building the segments of autonomy that are too low.

TNTs to Boost Autonomy

In addition to some of the bigger-picture thinking above, these are other ways for you to increase autonomy.

TNT: PROVIDE CONTEXT FOR RULES & GOALS

It's important to give your team the rationale, explanation, strategic thinking, and/or backstory for assignments and policy or initiative changes.[89] This is the "why." I call it "showing your mental work." Doing this unlocks autonomy by providing clarity, more nuanced decision making, and meaning. And it allows the people on your team to exercise judgment about task direction. The person receiving the explanation also equates the "why" or the explanation to being valued.

You can give explanations and rationales by providing context for decisions, rules, and changes; clearly articulating the potential benefits and positive outcomes associated with a rule or change; clearly outlining the expectations, requirements, and implications associated with a rule or change; keeping consistent open lines of communication; and providing updates, adjustments, and evaluations. Transparency is key.

TNT: EMPOWER DECISION MAKING

Team members need to be allowed to make choices about how they pursue their goals and to know the parameters around which they can make decisions about their work. Leaders must provide a clear framework for how a team is to operate when assigning projects or other responsibilities. Your team must know how to answer the following questions:[90]

1. What types of decisions do I/we have sole control to make? (Level 1 Decisions).
2. What types of decisions can I/we make but must also inform leadership? (Level 2 Decisions).
3. What types of decisions am I/we not allowed to make? (Level 3 Decisions).

Leaders need to be very clear about each of these questions and what their comfort level is, without micromanaging. You might not feel comfortable letting someone new to the organization or new to their career make Level 1 Decisions. Having the ultimate in decision-making latitude needs to be earned. At the same time, this is a process with a learning curve. Establishing clear timelines and dead-lines, explaining the level of resources and support available, trans-parency and sharing of information, and co-creating a check-in schedule will help the entire team better understand how they can proceed.

TNT: GET EVERYONE ON THE SAME PAGE

Effective teams are consistently on the same page about direction, priorities, and roles.[91] If you asked everyone on your team to explain the direction of a project, what has priority, and what each person's role is in executing deliverables, would they all give you the same answer? Your team should regularly discuss and have a clear under-standing of what success looks like and what are top priorities, with clear role clarity. Teams can then take control of and feel ownership over their actions. In addition, this strategy also enhances the "C" of the ABC needs.

It's easy to feel stuck and frustrated trying to figure out how to give your employees that freedom of choice. My goal with this seg-ment is to help you realize that you likely have more levers to push than you think to boost the autonomy needs of your team.

Now on to belonging.

Belonging: Rebuild Connection & Teaming

Relatedness, community, connection, and belonging collectively form the "B" in the ABC model. Belonging is the need to feel con-nected to others, to feel like you are part of groups that are impor-tant and significant to you, to feel cared about and cared for, and to create strong relationships. Cultivating strong connections among work teams is also strongly correlated with meaningful work and mattering.[92] Belonging should feel like this sentiment expressed by the chair of the antitrust litigation practice at a large West Coast-based law firm. He posted the following on LinkedIn: "Yesterday we ended the third week of the most intense trial I've had in my career—with a few days still to go next week. And we spent the evening watching the great *My Cousin Vinny* as a team over pizza and beer. That time together was as important as all the other hours we have poured into this trial. Not only is it vital to disconnect from work for a while during such intense periods—but perhaps nothing is more rejuvenating than time spent bonding with those we care about."[93]

But how do you do that in a distributed workforce? What does "community" even mean in the workplace today?

Conversations about community, what it should look like and how to build it given the way work is done now, are the subject of many of my workshop debriefs. Lack of community, you'll recall, is one of the Core 6 drivers of chronic stress and disengagement at work. The word that I often repeat is "intentionality." There continues to be a lack of intentionality around how workplace teams team, how friendships and community are formed, and how people generally can and should interact at work.

Leverage Moments That Matter & Workplace Friendships

While there is no one-size-fits-all approach for how to create community, individual free-for-all approaches don't work either. New research points to the importance of leveraging "moments that matter." The following moments that matter are pivotal times that open the door to intentional community building:[94]

1. **Team development opportunities.** Get people together three to four times per year, using a 50/50 mix of social and business interaction.
2. **Onboarding and training events.** These are good opportunities to get to know people better and create diverse, interconnected networks.

3. **New team formation and major initiative kickoffs.** Talking about team norms is a great way to accelerate community.
4. **Key moments for different parts of the organization.** Let senior leaders in different groups (e.g., sales and marketing, IT, design and engineering) work together to figure out specific moments that matter for their groups.

In addition to identifying key moments that matter as pivotal opportunities to develop community and connection, leaders must now rethink how to develop relationships with each other at work. In an era of increasing loneliness, work can be a powerful source of friendships. It has been shown that friendship groups outperform acquaintance groups on a variety of tasks—whether it's a more thinking-type cognitive task or a hands-on model-building task.[95] Friendship groups communicate better during a project and provide positive encouragement throughout. Decades-long research by Gallup has shown that if you have a best friend at work, you are more likely to engage your customers, get more done in less time, have a safe workplace with fewer accidents, and innovate and share ideas. Unfortunately, only 30% of employees report having a best friend at work, but those who do are seven times more likely to be engaged in their job.[96]

One team I worked with started an interest group about traveling as several employees mentioned it as a fun hobby. They meet monthly to discuss their upcoming trips, share best travel practices, and more. Their group continues to grow as word gets out within the organization. Another company I talked to established a lunch fund and strongly encouraged people to go lunch together once a month (in-person or virtually). The evolution and growth of friendships at work is a critical part of a healthy workplace.

TNTs to Boost Belonging

TNT: SCHEDULE UNSTRUCTURED TIME

Reserve time in 1:1s to talk about "nothing." The act of talking about nothing can be quite powerful, particularly when done consistently over time. A senior leader in a manufacturing organization told me that he calls these "well-being check-ins." Every two weeks he meets with his team members 1:1 for about 20 minutes to ask them about their life. He noticed a tremendous difference not only in his team's well-being, but also in the level of trust they have with each other and their willingness to talk about a variety of topics. One chief HR officer from a medical software company makes "15-minute heart-beat" calls, and she uses them just to get people in sync and to check in. To get started, instead of asking, "How are you doing?" which usually elicits a response of "fine" and thus halts the conversation, ask questions like the following:[97]

- What has your attention right now?
- What kind of day have you had?
- What do you need help with today/this week/short term?
- What has been most meaningful to you today/this week?

These questions feel a little less invasive and let the person choose whether to answer with work-related or home-related answers (or both).

Also make sure that your larger team meetings, offsites, and retreats include plenty of unstructured time (without a business outcome associated with it) to allow for people to continue to get to know each other and to just *be*.

In addition, moments of unstructured time help quiet your mind, giving it a rest from having to perform structured, productive tasks.[98] That leaves room for the creative-thinking part of your brain to emerge. That's why you have some of your best ideas in the shower (or while doing dishes, folding laundry, or running)!

TNT: OFFER OPPORTUNITIES TO INCLUDE EMPLOYEES' FRIENDS & FAMILY

I wrote extensively about my work with the US military in my first book. After I finished my master's degree in applied positive psychology, I spent almost four years as part of the University of

Pennsylvania's faculty teaching senior military personnel a version of the Penn Resilience Program. During that time, I had the unique opportunity to help pilot a version of the training for military spouses. The men and women who formed our inaugural cohort at Fort Campbell in 2012 remain my favorite group of people I have ever taught. The initiative was spearheaded by Maria McConville, wife of then base commanding officer General James C. McConville (who most recently served as the 40th Chief of Staff of the Army, retiring in 2023). What made that cohort so special was the eagerness and earnestness that these spouses brought to the course. They saw stress and well-being concerns with a very different perspective.

Since then, I have suggested that companies in all industries should more broadly extend their well-being programing to family members of employees. Employees who do not have a spouse or significant other should be allowed to designate a close family member or friend. While a spouse might have access to a company employee assistance program, what I'm talking about is something different. Workshops, on-demand content, mental health first aid training and other certification opportunities should extend to an employee's designated person. Why? An employee's "close other" sees stress and well-being challenges more closely and often, more intimately and differently than a leader or person in one's work universe. Second, it's a huge belonging signal to include friends and family in this and other ways. Many people have complicated lives, and the stress from both work and life domains can blend. Employees want work and life to be more integrated, and this is one pathway to achieve this.

Another pathway involves sharing positive workplace events with your friends and family.

TNT: SHARE POSITIVE WORKPLACE EVENTS WITH YOUR FAMILY & FRIENDS

Active Constructive Responding (ACR) is a skill that helps you build and maintain strong relationships by capitalizing on others' good news. It is one of my favorite skills to teach. Newer research explores the intersection of work-family integration and interpersonal capitalization in a way that offers a bit of a fresh take on why this skill is important. Work-family interpersonal capitalization is an active response process to positive work events that involves sharing or discussing such events with your partner, spouse, friends, or a close "other." You can use this skill yourself, but also make sure to take time to let your team know how valuable it is to share good workplace news outside of work.

Responses to good news must be both active and constructive (rather than passive and destructive) to build relationships, and each response style has certain characteristics.[99] Included in Table 4.2 is an example of each type of response to the good news—you just got promoted—you are telling your significant other.

Researchers discovered that sharing positive workplace experiences with your family or close "others" boosts both the work and home sides of the engagement equation. The exercise increased not

Table 4.2. Response Styles to Good News

Active Constructive ("Joy Multiplier")	Active Destructive ("Joy Thief")
• The responder asks questions and additional details. • They also ask about the underlying meaning of the event. *Sounds like*: "Congratulations! I'm so proud of you! How should we celebrate?"	• The responder points out negative implications. • The event's significance is minimized. *Sounds like*: "Well, that sounds great, but isn't that going to mean more responsibility and longer working hours? I hardly see you enough as it is."
Passive Constructive ("Faux Listener")	**Passive Destructive ("Response Shifter")**
• Very little is said. • The good news is acknowledged but there may be silence. *Sounds like*: "That's great!"	• The good news is ignored altogether. • The responder changes the subject or directs the conversation to something else about him or her. *Sounds like*: "Oh wow! That reminds me, I need to go finish my grocery list."

Note: *The terms "Joy Multiplier" and "Joy Thief" in the table were coined by Karen Reivich and used as part of the University of Pennsylvania team's instruction of this skill to US Army personnel as part of the Army's Comprehensive Solider and Family Fitness program.*

only work engagement but also family satisfaction and family well-being (through spillover effects—my positive mood from work spills over into and impacts my after-work life).[100] In addition, positive affect increased, as did life satisfaction.[101] The actual sharing of the good news adds to the beneficial effects of positive work events on employee well-being.

Good belonging practices start with intentionality. Now on to ABC need #3, challenge.

Challenge: Reinforce Opportunities for Learning & Growth

Challenges are those activities that ignite your desire to test your strengths and abilities and give you an opportunity to improve. People need to and want to be challenged and to experience growth at work, and that's not happening with near enough frequency. Recent data from the Microsoft Work Trend Index shows that 56% of employees and 68% of business decision makers say there are not enough growth opportunities in their own company to make them want to stay long term. In addition, two out of three employees say they would stay at a company longer if it were easier to change jobs internally. That rises to three in four for people managers and to 77% for decision makers.[102] Workers across age ranges have expressed dissatisfaction about workplace training opportunities, with data revealing that 57% of surveyed employees are pursuing training outside of work because they do not believe that company training programs teach them relevant skills, advance their career development, or help them stay competitive.[103]

In Gallup's 2023 *State of the Global Workplace* report, researchers asked this question: "What would you change about your workplace to make it better?" Forty-one percent of respondents answered "engagement or culture." Within that segment, one of the most frequently cited sentiments was, "I would like to learn more things, but the work I do is quite repetitive."[104]

Creating a Culture of Learning, Development, & Growth

Many leaders I work with express hesitation about fully investing money toward educating, upskilling, and reskilling their teams. They are hesitant to spend significant dollars in an area that may yield little return if the employee decides to leave the organization. This is short-sighted thinking. Yvette Ostolaza explained that Sidley thinks of its Built to Lead program as a true investment in the future. She realizes that not all Sidley lawyers who complete this program will stay at Sidley. Her perspective is that Sidley wants to train people to be phenomenal leaders wherever they go, hoping they will give back to their organizations and communities along the way. Ultimately, the firm wants its lawyers to have learned best practices that will be critical as the legal profession evolves. In the short time that the program has been in existence, the firm has received glowing testimonials from attendees. While Sidley will continue to measure the program's success, Yvette shared that it's already been a valuable talent attraction tool. And most recently, *Time* magazine included Sidley in its list of the best companies for future leaders, the only law firm to make the list.[105]

TNTs to Boost Challenge

Organizations of all sizes and across industries can follow Sidley's lead. Institutions of higher learning can be valuable partners to help bridge the learning and development gaps that might exist. Many organizations now have internal coaches or access to external coaching resources, and I have found that coaching is a critical aspect of helping people retain and implement what they have learned, particularly in the well-being and work psychology space.

TNT: DEVELOP A FRAMEWORK TO RESKILL/UPSKILL

Reskilling and upskilling are both processes designed to help employees learn new skills. Reskilling helps employees learn new skills so they can pivot into new roles if their current roles become obsolete or less relevant, while upskilling helps employees gain new skills to improve their current role or advance in their careers, often within their organization. The impact of technology on jobs is not new, but GenAI is disruption on a different level. Despite some of the initial rhetoric about GenAI, employees overall report feeling aware, but unafraid, of tech disruption. Approximately 50% of employees anticipate that some of their tasks will change, and that these changes will require new skills, while about 20% feel their job will be transformed to a point where significant reskilling will be required.[106]

Here is a short four-step process to help you frame your reskilling and/or upskilling efforts:

- **Step 1**: Assess where you and your team are at now.
  - What skills do you currently have?
  - What skills are needed now, and what skills will be needed in the future?
  - Where are the gaps? What upskilling and reskilling needs do you have in the immediate short term? Regular skills audits will help you stay on top of needs. What GenAI tools can help your efforts?
- **Step 2**: Create a learning development plan and set clear goals.
  - What are the specific objectives that your reskilling or upskilling programs will accomplish?
- **Step 3**: Consider the different learning methods to best help you accomplish your goals.[107]
  - Higher education: utilize traditional universities, tech or vocational schools, experiential learning.
  - Company-sponsored training: in-house workshops, seminars, and training sessions led by internal experts or external consultants.
  - Online courses and certifications: utilize self-study open-course programs.
  - Mentorship and coaching: include opportunities for reverse mentorship.

○ Job rotation: Can you work in different roles or departments to gain additional experience and skills?
• **Step 4**: Monitor and evaluate progress and adjust as needed.

TNT: IDENTIFY PATHWAYS FOR MASTERY EXPERIENCES

To continue to meet additional challenges and to build the confidence your team needs to accept harder projects and grow, you will need to help them develop a mindset of confidence and growth. This mindset of confidence and growth is called "self-efficacy" or "efficacy," and it exists at the individual and team level.[108] Your team members won't feel comfortable taking on new challenges or feel like they can grow within their career the way they want to if they don't first think they're up to the challenge.

Efficacy is the belief in your ability to cope with a broad range of stressful or challenging demands and to succeed.[109] Individuals with high self-efficacy are more likely to persevere, set courses of action that are personal and meaningful, and commit to challenging goals and good risks.[110] Efficacy is usually context- or domain-specific. You might feel highly confident about giving presentations at work but less confident about parenting a teenager. The good news about efficacy, though, is it's sticky. As you learn new skills and master new challenges, your beliefs about your skills and capabilities generally increase, permanently changing what you believe you (and your team) are capable of.

The most effective way to help people on your team increase their efficacy in a particular area is to learn by doing. You need to help them seek out "mastery experiences"—opportunities to try the skill or capacity that they find challenging or are trying to learn more about. For example, if your direct report wants to increase their public speaking efficacy, then you need to help them look for opportunities to speak more. Ask them to lead a team meeting, give a formal presentation, or record a training video. Or, if someone wants to improve their business acumen, then help them learn to read financial documents. Maybe suggest or otherwise greenlight money they can use toward a certificate course or additional learning. Whatever they choose, you both need to make sure that skill is practiced regularly.

TNT: THEN THINK WITH A GAMING MINDSET

Did you ever play video games as a kid? Or as an adult? What other games do you like to play and why? Growing up, I was obsessed with Pac-Man and Frogger. My parents had to put limits on my gaming because, as a competitive human, I would sit there for hours otherwise, trying to figure out how to conquer the most difficult levels to get to the end. And despite my parents' strict rules, my mom will be the first to admit that she had to wear a leather glove on her joystick hand because she developed blisters from playing so much. Games generally (and game theory) are a wonderful way to think about enhancing the ABC need of challenge.

Most every type of game, video games in particular, builds in elements that prominently and importantly support feelings of challenge. As you help your teams develop the skills they want to master or enhance, here are the elements that need to be present for them to stay motivated:[111]

1. **You need a clear goal.** When you play a game, rarely is there ambiguity about what is required to get ahead. You need to score more runs, points, or take a specific path to get to the next level. You need to either create the clear goal or make sure that your team is clear about exactly what needs to be done to "win."
2. **Include leveling.** Workers need to experience competence feedback as they achieve incremental goals and move to a higher level. This is part of the structure of Sidley's Built to Lead program. As associates progress through the program, they are given new titles, new capacities are acknowledged, and they gain access to new tools, such as coaching.

3. **Increase challenge difficulty, with some variety.** While it's true that your teams will need to work on and seek out challenges that continue to push them to develop their skills and strengths, every now and again it's nice to let them work on something that isn't the world's most difficult task.

4. **Offer loads of feedback.** One of the reasons why feedback is so important at work is that it activates ABC needs. Effective games are full of positive feedback. The "crowd" cheers; points increase; and lights, bells, and whistles deploy. If only you experienced positive feedback at work with the same immediacy (and excitement)! People need to know they are on the right path when they undertake a challenge, and often receive feedback, especially positive feedback, too infrequently.

Organizations cite skills gaps as a top barrier preventing industry transformation, with three-quarters of CEOs being concerned about how the availability of key skills will impact their growth strategies.[112] That means that the challenge and growth aspect of the ABC needs has become a critical future focus. Six out of 10 workers will require training before 2027, but only half of workers believe they have access to adequate training opportunities today.[113] As reskilling and upskilling become imperative, most of the needs for it are focused in cognitive and human-centered areas. The highest priorities for skills training from 2023 to 2027 are analytical thinking and creative thinking. GenAI-related training comes in third, followed by leadership training and resilience, flexibility, and agility skills.[114]

There are six aspects of work that are critically important to employees, and leaders consistently overlook (and underemphasize) their importance. I listed all six in chapters 1 and 3, but four of the six involve ABC needs: having caring and trusting teammates, potential for advancement, flexible work schedules, and a sense of belonging.[115] ABC needs represent the core pathways to improve your team's engagement and motivation. The time to start growing these capacities is now.

Lead Well: Ideas to Remember

- The ABC needs are a powerful trio that ignite engagement, motivation, and thriving in your workplace. They are autonomy, belonging, and challenge.
- Leaders need to be aware of the tension that workplace policies create within the ABC needs, specifically between autonomy and belonging, and find intentional ways to develop both.
- You now have a variety of ways to address all three of these needs via the different TNTs offered in this chapter. Make sure you ask your team members to be part of these discussions.

Chapter 5

Mindset #3
Create Workload Sustainability

Having a good work-life balance is one of the workplace characteristics people most value.[116] And one factor that makes it consistently difficult is having an unmanageable workload. In chapter 2, I introduced you to a large professional services firm that asked for my help to create more sustainable work practices. What we uncovered is an example of why trying to address this issue can be so complicated. The unmanageable workload issue was not happening equally across the organization. Most of it was happening on the project team, so implementation of next steps needed to be wide in some cases and targeted in others. Team norming practices were supposed to be followed at the outset of each project within the organization, and this was happening on an ad hoc basis. Team norming practices were intended to help teams get on the same page about how to work together, team values, how to communicate with each other, and what process to follow if work exceeded capacity. So, an easy first step was to start reintegrating team norming practices within the project team, as the problem was most acute there. We knew it would take at least several months to infuse new habits because of how burned out this team had become.

From there, we pulled together a small group of professionals representing all the different teams in the organization. We first talked about what was causing the unsustainable workload. The working group identified nearly 20 reasons why work overload occurred and decided to focus on the following four issues:

1. Lack of boundaries
2. Work scope was increasing
3. Work complexity was increasing
4. Work overload from other teams shifted to the project team

The working group then decided to pilot these ideas to help:

- Conduct a meetings audit to reduce unnecessary meetings.
- Improve communication practices (the working group would determine specifically what that meant on future calls).
- Clarify all roles and responsibilities to address job scope issues.
- Create and implement specific project team norms, and make sure those norms included setting boundaries.

As this case study illustrates, while leaders tend to look myopically at headcount as the only way to solve this problem, unmanageable workloads expose outdated teaming practices that simply adding more people won't fix—process and procedural issues like bad meeting practices, having too many meetings, loose or nonexistent job descriptions, bad or outdated or no systems, no boundaries, failure to create team norms, and inefficient communication. These are the issues that leaders have more control, influence, and leverage to address. Leaders also have control over how well they support their teams. If overloaded employees work for a leader that is encouraging, inspiring, and caring, they are less likely to suffer from burnout.[117] In addition, leader support becomes an important job resource that can increase job engagement, even when job demands are high.[118]

Alleviating work overload is a multifaceted process; however, I think it's critical for teams to take up this challenge because creating workload sustainability is *the* well-being challenge for organizations to address. The problem is too pervasive to ignore if you want to have an engaged and healthy team. According to one recent workplace well-being report, workload was identified as a key challenge by 44% of respondents in education, 47% of those in health-care, 48% of those looking to leave their job, and 63% of those experiencing burnout.[119]

Getting to the Root Causes of Work Overload & Overcommitment

Continuing with an important theme of this book, achieving work-load sustainability requires addressing the root causes of the problem. When work teams get stretched too thin, they become more reactive. Teams can't engage deeply with each other, and it makes it harder for them to create innovative solutions to the complex challenges you face. Teams also experience too many coordination costs—the constant need to keep bringing each other up to speed on projects.[120]

Why does work overload happen? Research points to the following causes:[121]

1. **Impact blindness.** Executive teams can lose track of the number and cumulative impact of the initiatives they have in progress, and then lack the ability to stop initiatives that aren't working.
2. **Limited line of sight.** Senior leaders can see their own teams' projects but have a more limited view of other groups' priorities.
3. **Under-resourced initiatives.** Senior leaders ask their teams to accomplish tasks without the requisite funding to make them happen.
4. **Band-Aid initiatives.** Too many projects provide limited fixes to significant problems, none of which address root causes.
5. **Failing to rebalance when people leave.** Organizations let people go without cutting the related work.

In addition, leaders must ensure that new hires are properly onboarded, workload assignment and tracking procedures are followed, and lack of trust isn't preventing team members from speaking up when they find themselves overloaded.[122] And, importantly, leaders need to examine whether the organizational culture promotes overwork. Many leaders have said some version of this to me: "We don't think about capacity in the leadership ranks; we work around the clock—it's part of our DNA; there's always a high sense of urgency; and we don't take our foot off the gas. Overwork is often rewarded."

How does your organization fare? Here are five yes/no questions for you to consider:[123]

- Are projects launched without coordination across units and functions?
- Are initiatives launched without a clear stopping point or end point?
- Are people expected to absorb new demands without stopping past projects?
- Are projects launched without success metrics?
- Does the organization lack a central group that reviews all current initiatives?

Your answers can point you to opportunities for finetuning your approach. Consider the questions below—it's an exercise I often use with teams and leaders.

TNT: SUGGESTIONS & KEY QUESTIONS TO ASK

- When do key workload surge and crunch times happen? What does each person have on his or her plate, and what are competing priorities?
- Is there a technology solution you're missing that would help?
- What repetitive tasks and processes can be made into templates, blueprints, flowcharts, or short video tutorials? Where will these materials live?

- How can you make information self-serve—that is, where can it be kept for all to access? This can reduce the need for unnecessary meetings.[124]
- Can you charge your clients more for last-minute requests? If I buy something online, and I want it next day, I must pay more (often, quite a bit more) than if I selected standard shipping. Leaders usually have mixed (and strong) opinions when I offer this as a strategy, but it may be something to consider.

All of this must be communicated clearly within your work team. Having well-established communication practices and strong relationships will make it easier to make the tough decisions that might be required to bring workload into a more sustainable range.

Workload Sustainability Starts with Better Communication & Strong Relationships

Client expectations are often cited as a major driver of stress and poor work environments. Every party has a role to play in addressing workload challenges and fostering a healthier way of working, and most of the "way we work" practices lack intentionality. Leaders at all levels of an organization must get better at organizing and communicating work priorities, but, given the volume of work in many organizations and a service-focused mindset that is expected to be preserved, teams and their clients don't often talk about the true expectations each has for producing great work and what exceptional client service means.

The Mindful Business Charter (MBC) and the U.S. Bank Guidelines (Guidelines) are examples of frameworks for establishing these intentional communication practices and relationships between teams and their clients. The outcome of deploying these frameworks is a less stressful, more intentional, and healthier way of working.

The MBC was launched in 2018 in the United Kingdom (UK) and included three banks—Barclays, Lloyds Bank, and the Royal

Bank of Scotland, along with nine of their outside vendors. Since the launch, there are now more than 140 members of the business community, many still heavily concentrated in the UK, who have signed on to follow MBC practices.[125] At the same time the MBC was created, U.S. Bank was also creating its own framework to establish better communication practices with its internal and external partners.

Ben Carpenter, U.S. Bank's deputy vice president and general counsel, was instrumental in helping the Guidelines come to fruition. When I talked to him about the intent of the Guidelines, he was clear: "This is not about taking our foot off the gas or resting more often. This is about working together to be healthier and ultimately improving the results."[126] I asked him, though, how the Guidelines actually get implemented. I assumed that many external partners or vendors would want to differentiate themselves by providing exceptional service (which usually means drop what you're doing and respond now in their minds) and would therefore feel uncomfortable initiating a conversation about this framework. Ben said that a partner or vendor does not have to sell a well-being message—they can use the Guidelines as a way to discuss how to build better relationships and deliver better results. He said outside vendors and clients can frame it this way: "We take care of our people, and we know that our people are at their best when everyone understands expectations around urgency and how you specifically want to grow and develop the relationship." This framing will work for your internal clients and partners too.

Importantly, Ben emphasized that the Guidelines aren't *rules*—they are meant to be a starting point to having a better conversation about making work better. Ben admitted that it's a work in progress because the mindset of "do it now" is so engrained and it's hard to shift, but he said the goal is for all the parties to get incrementally better, and he knows that's happening.

Table 5.1 shows the four pillars that make up the Guidelines, along with suggested practices for each pillar.

As a former practicing lawyer (and recovering skeptic), I know how entrenched the mindset of client responsiveness can be. The

Table 5.1. U.S. Bank Guidelines: Pillars & Suggested Practices

Pillar	Suggested Practices
Mindful communication with each other	• Be considerate of others during off hours. Consider delaying nonurgent communications until work hours. • The method of communication (call, email, text) and design (summaries, bullets, memos) should correspond with the relevant circumstances and the parties' preferences.
Work-life balance	• Manage professionals' workload appropriately based on their availability and urgency of the matter. • Urgent matters should be the exception, not the rule. Be clear about deadlines and timeline expectations.
Intentional project management	• Work together on issues and concerns prior to raising them with business line clients. • Work together to minimize issues related to billing and invoicing practices.
Joint programming opportunities	• Leverage outside vendor/client well-being events, initiatives, and activities. • We all have a shared common goal to promote well-being in our industry/profession.

expectation to always be on, and to pivot at a moment's notice regardless of plans, is real. While I work across industries, I rarely see that level of client service ethos displayed to such a near fanatical degree as I do in the legal profession. Given that law firms are an instrumental constituency of both frameworks, I wanted to talk to a lawyer in a large law firm to *really* understand if using a model like the Guidelines is even feasible. Mike Kraut is a partner at one of the world's largest law firms, Morgan Lewis & Bockius LLP. When I talked to him, I was most surprised to hear him say that not only have the Guidelines helped him enhance his teaming practices, but they have also been incorporated into basic client onboarding.[127]

When talking to new clients, Mike will ask them about their preferred billing methods and best practices for communication. After that initial discussion, pitching the pillars supporting the Guidelines becomes a more natural part of the conversation and an easier sell. He believes that the degree to which clients embrace well-being sits on a spectrum, and one needs to be aware of where that position is.

Some clients may expect immediacy in everything—then that's what must happen—but most do not. It requires developing the relationship to have these types of "how are we going to work together" conversations and also observing each client's behavior. During our conversation, Mike made an interesting point, one that I had not thought of. He said it very rarely occurs to service providers that hyper-responsiveness may not always be what the client wants or needs. He said, "When you send a client an email late at night in an effort to demonstrate to them that their matter is top of mind for you, while some might be impressed with that, a lot of them will not be. The reality is that you pinged them [at night] while perhaps they are watching TV with their family, and now, because of your email, they are thinking about a [work-related issue] they had put aside when they left work for the day."

Mike also shared that he has learned the value of making sure clients know his team. As a leader, internal or external clients may call you first or see you as the go-to person, but they also need to be comfortable with others on the team. Not only does that create better opportunities for your team members to gain valuable experience interacting with clients, but it also gives your client another attachment point. Mike is the first to admit he is a work in progress in this area. While he was away for his daughter's graduation weekend, he took a short client call between activities, but he felt it was the right thing to do as it was a new client and an urgent matter.

Further, Mike models the Guidelines for his internal team, which he believes increases trust, comfort, and psychological safety. He knows he's more interesting to his team (and to clients) if he has outside interests, family, and other pursuits, and talks about those things. That way, when a team member wants to leave early to attend their child's sporting event, for example, he celebrates that and talks about how much time he spent coaching Little League. He wants other people at the firm to want to work on the matters he leads. He sees his junior team members as either future leaders at the firm or future clients if they choose to leave the firm. Either way, he wants them to be bought into the same culture he believes in and is trying to build.

Ultimately, Mike sees the Guidelines as a great talent retention tool. He told me, "I'm usually on the 6:20 P.M. train at night. I start my day as early as I need to in order to be on the 6:20 P.M. train. Early on in my career, I found a way to [integrate work and family] in a way that works for my family and me. If your team has those same values, and you can't make home and life work, people will leave their job. So, finding ways to allow people to have the work experience that you and they want and the family life they want is the only way to keep talented people."

TNT: CREATE GOOD TEAMING PRACTICES—PART 1

Good teaming practices can help make workload more sustainable. I introduced the TNT of "Getting People on the Same Page" in chapter 4, and I want to build on that here. Specifically, it's important to build a shared, accurate, and complementary understanding of the knowledge, skills, and information the team possesses. There are several ways to build this shared understanding—here are a few:[128]

- **Path 1: Create a team charter.** Think about the purpose the Guidelines serve. They are meant to create a common understanding for "how we operate around here" about a specific topic—in this case, well-being. What is your team's mission, its objectives/goals and boundaries, and how are you going to operate together? What are your expectations about communication? You can create a charter for an ongoing team, or a project charter for a specific piece of work.
- **Path 2: Cross-train team members.** Mike said that while he's the point person, other people on his team interact with clients and know details of each matter. You can train others to fully fill in for you (full cross-training), train them to help out on a few tasks (partial cross-training), or to learn enough about what you do so they're simply more aware (interpositional knowledge training).

- **Path 3: Debriefs and huddles.** These are moments that allow you to update and transfer knowledge within the team or from team to team (common in healthcare as shifts change). Debriefs are great at the end of a project and allow your team to discuss what went well, what you would do differently, and what was unexpected.

Having these processes in place can accelerate a new hire's understanding of his or her role within the team, along with expectations so that the learning curve can be shortened.

I can understand if this feels like doing extra work when you're already overloaded and too busy. But none of these practices require a lot of time, and the payoff is big. When everyone on the team shares a common understanding of the processes and each other's knowledge and skills, team-level effort increases (which boosts performance), teams are better coordinated when performing routine tasks, and they make faster and smarter adjustments.[129] I'll give you more good teaming practices in chapter 6.

Long Hours Impact Well-Being—Maybe?

Just how much influence, though, do long work hours have on well-being? The answer is more complicated and nuanced than you may think. It has long been assumed that long work hours impose a high cost to workers in terms of overall quality of life and reduced physical and mental health. And my own research supports this. In 2023, I conducted a survey study with American Law Media, which was sent to lawyers and legal professionals in the United States.[130] A total of 887 people responded to our various questions about their quantity of work and other aspects associated with high stress and burnout. More than 69% of the respondents said that they have so much work to do that it takes away from time with family and friends a few times a week or more. Nearly 70% said that they have so much work to do that it takes away time from hobbies and personal inter-

Table 5.2. The Impact of Stress

Statement	% Who Responded "Once a Week," "a Few Times a Week," or "Every Day"
I am overwhelmed by the amount of work I have	63.3%
I have a hard time concentrating at work	64.9%
I have become less interested in my work	63.4%
I have become more cynical about my work	68%
I feel emotionally drained on a regular basis from my work	68.7%

ests a few times a week or more. Table 5.2 is a summary of some of the effects they reported.

An analysis of the research shows that the effects of long work hours may vary considerably for different working populations based on age, working conditions, gender, and other factors, and that the relationship between work hours and well-being is weaker and less consistent than expected.[131] One study revealed that working during nonstandard work time may undermine intrinsic motivation because people are more likely to think about the other ways they could have spent their time—like having fun, spending time with friends or family, or something else.[132]

Two things can help limit this thinking. The first is to know your "why."[133] I spent many sunny weekends working on this book, but what helped me to avoid dwelling on what else I could have been doing—and to meet my deadlines—was believing that this material was needed to advance the workplace well-being conversation. So, if you find yourself frustrated about working at night and/or on the weekends, try to connect to the bigger picture or deeper reason or outcome for your work.

Second, whether you have autonomy or choice over the decision to work during off hours is key. According to Dr. Dave Whiteside, director of insights at YMCA WorkWell, the issue in creating healthy work environments is not working on the weekends or in the evening. Rather, it's feeling like you have no choice but to be working at a time when it's inconvenient for you to be working. I personally love working in the evenings after my daughter Lucy goes to bed. The house is quiet for a couple of hours, and I can do focused and concentrated work. Dave said, "We talk about these 'acceptable times' and 'unacceptable times' to work quite often, but giving people the full freedom to work when it is most convenient for their own personal needs is what healthy work really looks like."

Can GenAI Help?

Nearly two-thirds of workers say they struggle with having enough time and energy to do their job, with 68% saying they don't have enough uninterrupted focus time during the day and 62% saying they spend too much time tracking down information.[134] As such, 70% of employees would delegate as much work as possible to GenAI to reduce their workload.[135] However, the excitement about GenAI may be outpacing people's ability to learn these tools in a way that actually enhances productivity. One report found that 77% of employees say GenAI has actually added to their workload.[136] Separately, 79% of leaders believed their organizations needed to adopt GenAI to stay competitive, but 60% worried that their organization lacked a clear plan and vision to implement it.[137] Many employees feel burned out, which organizations need to address before they add new parameters for GenAI adoption. In the meantime, leaders can offer GenAI training programs that are tailored to different roles and give people adequate time for experimentation and learning.[138]

TNT: TRY THIS AI PROMPT

There are GenAI-related presentations at almost every conference I speak at, and when my travel schedule allows, I like to listen in for a variety of reasons. At one such program, the presenter shared a prompt she saw a colleague post on LinkedIn, and it resonated.

The colleague was using Microsoft's GenAI tool, Copilot, and this was her prompt sequence:[139]

I am trying to plan ahead for today. I'd like you to please act as my executive assistant and provide me with an overview of what is on my plate today. This is a combination of several smaller reports you will provide to me as part of an executive briefing.

- **Step 1:** Pull a list of all of my meetings for today.
- **Step 2:** Aggregate all of the meeting information into table format that I can easily read. The columns should be: "Time" | "Meeting Title."
- **Step 3:** Summarize my Teams chats and channels from today.
- **Step 4:** Go through my inbox and summarize my emails where I am in the "to" line and there is direct action required. Summarize into a table with the columns "Email Title" | "Email Summary" | "Recommended Action."
- **Step 5:** Based on the above, please suggest the top three actions I should focus on.

I encourage you to become familiar with the GenAI tools available at your organization. When implemented properly, I think these tools have the potential to help alleviate at least some of your digital overload.

Other TNTs to Create Workload Sustainability

TNT: ASSESS OPEN PROJECTS & INITIATIVES

In order to begin to alleviate work overload, you need to first figure out how many initiatives you have open; then assess each one as to business need, budget, personnel allocation, and business impact; establish priorities in an integrated way (getting input from various managers and leaders as needed); and establish a firm end date.[140] This takes time, but it's a critical first step.

TNT: CONDUCT A MEETINGS AUDIT

Software company Atlassian surveyed more than 5,000 knowledge workers around the world and found that meetings are the main reason they struggle to get their work done. In fact, meetings were considered ineffective 72% of the time.[141] Respondents cited the following reasons for this ineffectiveness (and I hear so many teams echo these same sentiments):

- There was a lack of clarity on next steps.
- We didn't need to meet—this could have been an email.
- It was conversational chaos—there was no structure to the meeting.
- A few people dominated the conversation.

And 78% of the respondents said that they attended so many meetings they found it hard to get their work done. Atlassian's Team Anywhere Lab decided to create a meetings experiment, and here are their recommendations for improving meetings:

- Have an explicitly stated goal.
- Have an agenda (yes, it takes time to create, but 79% of respondents said it helped make meetings more productive).
- Default to a standard length of 15 minutes.
- Engage a meeting facilitator to keep people on track and to ensure all voices are heard.
- Circulate a document ahead of time so people can add their thoughts, notes, and ideas (you might find that a meeting isn't even necessary if people share enough information this way).
- For updates and status, create a video and share the information in a video message instead.

TNT: TIMEBOX YOUR PRIORITIES

Atlassian conducted a different experiment to help its teams figure out the right cadence for the type of work they had to complete. Their findings are as follows:[142]

- Meetings should take up about 30% of your week. Decline meetings that aren't critical (which might require that you fight your inner FOMO critic).
- Open collaboration should be about 10–20% of your week. Open collaboration is blocking off time when you know your key collaborators will be online.
- Focus time for deep work and deep thinking should represent 30–40% of your time.
- The last 20% or so of your time should be reserved for responding to messages. This reigns in the temptation to constantly respond to each notification you get in real time.

Having a high workload isn't necessarily a bad thing. It's good to feel needed and wanted at work, and it's good to be part of challenging work. What's not good is to consistently feel like you're treading water and that at any moment you might sink because you have so much to do.

Lead Well: Ideas to Remember

- Unsustainable workloads are one of the top well-being challenges for many organizations, and workload challenges require workload solutions.
- It's important for leaders to identify the root causes of workload and overcommitment. Those will have to be addressed to have success in this area.
- Don't be afraid to have conversations with your internal and external clients and customers about workload priorities. You

can use the U.S. Bank Guidelines as a starting point to frame the conversation about building good relationships and communication practices.

- Developing great teaming practices, timeboxing top priorities, conducting meetings audits, and other simple strategies can provide outsized stress relief to your team.

Chapter 6

Mindset #4
Build Systemic Stress Resilience

"Ugh, Paula, do we *really* need more resilience?" That was the question posed to me by a C-level leader at one of my round-table presentations, ironically focused on building more engaged and resilient teams.

I have been studying, teaching, writing, talking, and thinking about resilience since I first discovered the science of it in 2010 during my master's studies, and I wrote my master's thesis on the topic. I have seen countless lives and teams transformed by the power of resilience, including my own. Yet, for all its ubiquity, resilience is one of the most misunderstood concepts at work. It's also one of the most important, given the level of uncertainty and change that is and will continue to be present at work into the foreseeable future.

The research literature can also be confusing, because there are many definitions of resilience and most of them have a clinical or trauma-related focus rather than a work focus. In addition, popular media talks about resilience as though it's a superhuman capacity possessed only by Navy SEALs. Most definitions of resilience include these two themes:[143]

1. **Capacity.** Resilience is an individual's, team's, or organization's capacity to manage the small and large challenges, pressures, and stressors it faces.
2. **Growth.** Resilience is about both bouncing back *and* bouncing forward. Resilient individuals, teams, and organizations

learn valuable lessons from setbacks, obstacles, and stress, and apply those lessons to future challenges going forward to enhance agility.

Resilience, then, is defined here as an individual's, team's, or organization's capacity for stress-related growth. After many decades of research, we know that resilience is also not a fixed trait that you either have or don't have; rather, it's a set of skills that you can build.[144] Nor is it blind perseverance; it's perseverance *with a purpose*. When a challenge happens, big or small, you must evaluate whether you, your team, and your organization are pursuing the right course of action to manage it. If you are, stay the course. If you are not, the resilient response may be to pivot or to stop something altogether.

So, when a leader asks me very skeptically, "Paula, do we *really* need more resilience?" I ask in response: "Does your team need more skills and tools to better manage stress, adversity, and change, to make the best business decisions possible in those moments, and then learn and grow from those challenges so that your team can navigate future problems more quickly?" Almost every leader says, "Yes!" That's resilience—and individuals, teams, and organizations will need it in spades.

Unfortunately, resilience has become synonymous with many organizations' wellness efforts such that the concept is often viewed with an eye roll and not taken as seriously as it should be. Others may feel like there is an organizational hidden agenda to increase worker productivity or tolerance of unhealthy corporate cultures. As a result, the nuance of the concept, along with how it's related to other important business objectives, is also totally lost along with the business case. Individuals and organizations with higher levels of resilience are happier, healthier, and more successful in uncertain and changing environments, and companies with higher workforce resilience see 320% more year-over-year growth than those with lower levels.[145]

Research also shows that employees who are adaptable tend to have an edge when it comes to managing change and adversity—

adaptability acts as a buffer to the impact of workplace stress.[146] However, other findings show that it is misguided to see building individual resilience skills as the sole solution to workplace challenges because, as I have pointed out throughout the book, individual skills alone cannot fix an unsupportive or toxic work environment. In addition, while resilient employees are better able to work in more difficult work environments, they are less likely to tolerate them.[147] In fact, one survey showed that employees with high resilience and adaptability were 60% more likely to say they planned to leave their company if they experienced unfavorable work environments compared to those with lower levels of resilience and adaptability.[148]

Importantly, many qualities that support organizational resilience, like strong leadership and having good networks and relationships, also offer tangible benefits to the way an organization generally operates.[149] When people see resilience embedded and talked about as critical to good teaming, as a leadership skillset, and as a skillset to help the organization itself, it takes on new meaning. Companies shouldn't ask people to "be more resilient" if they are not first willing to address the very work environments that often make work more challenging than it needs to be. That's why the title of this chapter is so intentional: resilience needs to be prioritized across the workplace ecosystem, and I'm focusing on team and organizational resilience in this chapter.

Building Resilient Teams

I created a Resilient Teams Inventory in my first book to help teams begin a conversation about resilience and how to develop it. The Inventory questions track the model of team resilience and thriving I created called PRIMED. The expanded form of the acronym is as follows:

- P: Psychological Safety & Psychological Needs
- R: Relationships
- I: Impact

- M: Mental Strength
- E: Energy
- D: Design

Many leaders and teams have completed the Inventory. Of those I have received (many are kept by leaders and teams to continue the conversation), the average self-reported team resiliency score was 36.9 out of a highest possible score of 50. The average range was 19–45. Most teams found that they had some improvements to make.

The most poorly ranked statement, by far, was "We are alert to and respond to early signs of overload in team members." The second most common finding across teams and industries was that they struggled having difficult conversations with each other. This occurs for many reasons, but I find that many teams need to create a stronger foundation, and that starts with psychological safety and trust. And that's how I came to work with American Express.

A Story of Team Resilience from American Express

I first met Sarah Dodds-Brown in 2020. At the time, she led the US Business Legal Group at American Express, and she asked me to come speak to her team about psychological safety and resilient teaming. Sarah had read a *New York Times* article about Google's quest to build a perfect team, in which they discovered that it was psychological safety, more than anything else, that was critical to making a team work.[150] I could tell at the time that getting teaming right was important to her, and our paths crossed again in 2022 after she read my first book. Now in her role as Executive Vice President & Deputy General Counsel, she asked me again to speak to her new expanded team, which currently leads support for many strategic and cross-functional initiatives and provides expertise and advice across a range of global subject-matter and regulatory areas within American Express. My workshop on building resilient teams was meant to support the work her team had already started to do, and before I spoke, she invited me to sit in on a session she led with the team about the status of their ongoing efforts. It was a unique opportunity to see the initial stages and "behind the scenes" process of teaming, and it fascinated me. Fast-forward to today, and I knew I wanted to ask her more about how that process started.

She told me that American Express created a company-wide set of training modules—called "Building a Winning Team"—that were designed to help teams in different stages of formation.[151] The first module focused on building team norms: what they called "team cohesion." When she took over her current role in 2022, Sarah knew that the team generally needed help in this area. The subgroups that comprised her new larger team had been split and rebranded multiple times, and there had been a lot of leader turnover. The team generally had no real identity, and she knew she had to first create a sense of team identity and trust. Organizationally, she advocated for more resources for the team, which helped, but they also needed a mindset shift.

She first asked everyone on the team to complete one of the Building a Winning Team exercises. To start, nine cohorts, including people of all titles within the department, formed an in-depth plan to increase their team's effectiveness, guided by these five key differentiators common to high-performing teams:

1. **Trust:** Team members can take risks and share diverse perspectives without fear of negative consequences.
2. **Purpose:** Teams are committed to a clear and compelling purpose connected to the broader organization's mission and vision.
3. **Accountability:** Team members understand their individual responsibilities and expected contributions and seek out specific and actionable feedback to stay accountable.
4. **Adaptability:** Teams consistently assess, respond to, and learn from changes in the work environment.
5. **Cohesion:** Established working norms are followed and govern how teams interact, with transparency, feedback, and respect at the center.

The cohorts then compiled an exhaustive list of team norms: agreements about how team members would work with each other and how the team would work as a whole. The cohorts talked about operating principles for open communication, how to provide and receive feedback, how to foster inclusion, what it meant to be efficient with each other's time, and knowledge sharing. They made lists for each of these sections.

After approximately five months, the cohort groups reassembled to review how they were operating as to those norms. They discovered that giving each other feedback and having candid conversations was proving to be the biggest challenge. To increase team vulnerability and communication, Sarah created a short one-minute video and sent it to her team. In the video, she talked about a time when she received some unexpected feedback from a senior colleague and how the feedback, which startled her, led her to more deeply and intentionally think about the kind of leader she wanted to become. That video both demonstrated her own vulnerability and gave her team members parameters for their own sharing. She then asked team members to create their own one-minute stories of a time when they overcame a challenge to share with their cohorts, and she gave people the option to opt out. Most people chose to participate and found the process to be transformative.

Sarah told me that her team has pushed her, hard at times, to justify how and why concepts like vulnerability and psychological safety relate to their core work, as many on her team felt their substantive knowledge alone was enough to be effective in their work efforts. Her framing back to them was spot on. She told them that creating a psychologically safe team would become the training ground for showing vulnerability, taking risks to deliver and receive feedback, and having difficult conversations so that it would become easier to deliver difficult messages to the business and other stakeholders in arenas where the stakes were much higher. She calls the result "psychological courage." Psychological safety and having a cohesive team is not, for her, the end game for her team. She needs people on her team to feel comfortable showing up in rooms where they may need to give advice to senior leaders who are unhappy with or disagreeing with advice or positioning, or point out the elephant in the room, or say the thing that needs to be said that others might not want to hear. Being able to do that in the context of their own team first makes it easier to have those conversations when the stakes may be much higher and more unforgiving.

Team trust, vulnerability, and psychological safety, building toward the ultimate goal of psychological courage, are now foundational principles embedded into the culture of Sarah's team. In order to make sure these principles are lived, Sarah holds regular skip-level meetings and periodic town halls to reinforce them. She also expects both new and senior members of the team to live these values. She calls her team coordinated and resilient.

A big reason why I suspect Sarah was so successful in this endeavor is that she went first and modeled the behavior she wanted to see. Research has shown that leader-demonstrated vulnerability matters dramatically to psychological safety. Leaders often seek feedback from their team members, but this can be the wrong approach because conversations often dissolve into defensiveness or inaction. However, when leaders openly shared criticisms or suggestions they had received about their own performance, team members then felt safer to share their own challenges, thus opening the type of conversations leaders desired in the first place.[152] For psychological safety to endure, leaders must model this vulnerability and receptivity first.

Research has begun to identify more clearly what it takes for teams to cope, and even flourish, when they experience change and uncertainty.[153] Specifically, resilient teams, both in-person and virtual, draw on four important resources:[154]

- **Team efficacy.** They are collectively confident that even in the face of adversity, they can deliver whatever is needed to get the job done. I talk about the importance of efficacy in chapter 4.

- **Clear roles and responsibilities.** They have previous or established interaction patterns and are familiar with each other's knowledge, skills, and preferences (not easy when teams have lots of turnover or continuously disband and reform with new people).
- **Improvisation.** I think of this as the MacGyver principle. Resilient teams can use their existing resources to develop something new, and they are able to pivot quickly to Plan B or Plan C if necessary (or to stop a course of action that isn't working).
- **Psychological safety.** The shared belief that it is safe for team members to take interpersonal risks like delivering hard feedback, asking difficult questions, questioning a course of action or ideas, or proposing a novel idea for team members to consider.

In one of the most interesting studies I have read, it now appears as though a very strong factor in helping to predict whether teams make good decisions is the speed of everyone's heartbeat. Researchers used heart rate monitors to collect data during group discussions, focusing on heart rate synchrony as a measure of group cohesion and engagement. When heart rates were in stronger alignment, the group was more likely to reach the correct consensus and make the best decision, likely an indication of high psychological safety in the group.[155]

TNTs to Build Team Resilience

TNT: A ROADMAP FOR RESILIENCE BEFORE, DURING, & AFTER A CHALLENGE

It's important for teams to act intentionally before, during, and after a challenge. This roadmap will help your team increase its stress resilience by preparing in advance, reacting appropriately during the adversity, and then growing from it after.[156] I have outlined the tactical strategies for resilient collaboration in Table 6.1.

Table 6.1. Your Resilience Roadmap

Before	During	After
Anticipate challenges and plan contingencies.	Make real-time adjustments quickly if something isn't working.	Debrief: What went well? What do you need to improve?
Know team members' capacity levels (is a particular division operating beyond capacity such that it will impact its ability to help/respond effectively).	Reclarify roles and goals for teams that are required to meet remotely or in a hybrid format; disruptive events may create new and competing tasks for teams.	Address any friction points that may have emerged between team members.
Address known vulnerabilities (e.g., distrust among team members; lack of resources/ expertise).	Provide transparency and ongoing status updates to reduce ambiguity and enhance team members' efforts to manage it.	Communicate appreciation to team members (from both leaders and peers).
Establish a process for regular communication about a developing problem.	Continue constructive routines like regular meetings (but monitor meeting overload).	Thank external resources for their help and support.
Identify backups for people in key roles.	Tap into resources outside the team or organization to get others' insight/knowledge.	
	Keep it personal—don't forget about personal interaction and check-ins.	

TNT: DEBRIEF AFTER MICRO-CHALLENGES

Micro-challenges are small frustrations and setbacks that teams experience on a more regular basis than big adversities. Don't brush these aside. Research has demonstrated that how you recover from minor challenges is predictive of how you'll cope with bigger ones.[157] Use them as opportunities to deploy some of the strategies in Table 6.1. They will build your resilience muscles so that you're ready to flex when the big challenges hit. As I mentioned in chapter 5 and in Table 6.1, you can start by discussing what went well, what you would improve, and what specific actions helped or didn't help.

TNT: CREATE GOOD TEAMING PRACTICES—PART 2

I gave you several TNTs to create good teaming practices in chapter 5, and I want to build on those here because they are so important for resilience. At a foundational level, teams will struggle to respond effectively in an uncertain environment if they don't team well.

Atlassian is doing amazing work to understand more about good teaming practices.[158] I wrote about some of the practices they researched in chapter 5 to help craft better meetings and timebox your day. The company recently released its *State of Teams* report for which they surveyed 5,000 knowledge workers and 100 Fortune 500 executives to learn more about how teams were collaborating today. Atlassian discovered that among Fortune 500 companies alone, approximately 25 *billion* hours were lost each year due to ineffective teaming. The executives who were interviewed estimated that only 24% of their teams were doing mission-critical work. Why were they struggling?

1. Teams are spread across disjointed goals.
2. They are drowning in notifications and meetings.
3. Information they need to be effective is hard to find and not located in a central spot.
4. They are unsure how to leverage GenAI to help.

As a result, resilient teams need to act on and answer three questions:

Question 1: Are we working on the right things?

To help, teams must do the following:

a. Set clear goals.
b. Make goals visible to everyone by embedding them on a shared platform where they can be tracked.

   c. Create rituals that clarify priorities. This can be done by managers sharing weekly short video updates to increase goal clarity and team connection.

Question 2: Do we have time to make real progress?

To help, teams must do the following:

   a. Make calendars reflect priorities. Effective teams design their workdays around their highest-priority work (see chapter 5).

   b. Run better meetings (see chapter 5).

   c. Replace some meetings with asynchronous videos. Videos are easy ways to share updates, and people can process the information at their own pace. Atlassian experimented with this component whereby 43% of Atlassians had a meeting replaced by a video, and they found that it freed up approximately 5,000 hours of focus time collectively.

Question 3: Is knowledge easy to find and understand?

To help, teams must do the following:

   a. Pay attention to the quality of the documents your team produces. High-quality documents are concise, clearly articulated, and answer team members' questions. You can experiment with GenAI tools to help.

   b. Put documents on a shared platform that is easy to search and easily accessible for the entire team.

   c. Use GenAI to help make knowledge flow. GenAI can help your team create summary results, automate administrative work, and enable knowledge mining (and search).

Now consider if your team has even some of these structures in place. When both small and large adversities happen, it will be much easier to communicate with each other and to find the information you need to more easily.

As we have seen, team resilience is important, but what are the benefits of organizational resilience, and what are the important building blocks?

Building Resilient Organizations

When McKinsey surveyed more than 2,500 organizational leaders around the world in 2023, half of them stated that their organization was unprepared to react to future shocks.[159] That finding stunned me when I read it because the survey was released post-pandemic. The survey also found that in the 2020–2021 economic recovery, resilient organizations generated total shareholder return 50% higher than their less resilient peers.[160]

Organizations that are adaptable and resilient are better able to both absorb shocks and turn them into opportunities for growth, while organizations low in adaptability and resilience are both unmotivated to prepare for a crisis during moments of calm and unable to change course and react resiliently when disruption occurs.[161] In addition, there are important financial outcomes tied to adaptability. When organizations prioritize a culture of adaptability, they talk about it more in annual reports and their research and development expenditures increase over a three-year period compared to companies that don't foster a culture of adaptability.[162] In addition, those organizations that prioritized fostering a culture of adaptability achieved better financial performance over a three-year period.[163] BetterUp found that during the pandemic, companies with high workforce resilience had a 42% higher return on assets, a 3.7% higher annual return on equity, and 320% higher year-over-year growth, as I noted at the start of this chapter. They further found that employees who report to resilient leaders are less burned out, and teams with resilient leaders are more productive.[164]

While organizational resilience may seem like a must-have in these uncertain times, there are forces acting against establishing a culture of resilience. These include lack of money—too few dollars available to develop the necessary surplus capacity and contingency plans; lack of clarity about whether the organization prioritizes resilience; and, lastly, too many initiatives launched in silos, which limits their broader applicability and effectiveness.[165]

Pathways to Increase Organizational Resilience

There are several different pathways to increase organizational resilience:[166]

- Strong internal and external partnerships
- Strong leadership practices
- Sufficient resources—financial, operational, material, and technical
- Preparedness & planning—you practice and test plans at regular intervals to identify weaknesses and vulnerabilities
- Situational awareness
- Motivated and engaged workers; well-being is prioritized
- Innovation and creativity
- Decision-making adaptability—your organization can make tough decisions quickly

Research shows that of those items listed above, the following five are the most important:[167]

1. **Having strong leadership practices:** Your organization has leaders whom people trust and want to follow at every level. Leaders create a shared vision and are visible and available.
2. **Motivated workers:** Your people are engaged and work together as a connected team, and they are committed to working on a problem until it is resolved.

3. **Situational awareness:** You monitor your industry for early warning signs of emerging issues.
4. **Innovation:** Your organization values innovation and creativity, and you quickly fix and update processes that don't work.
5. **Effective partnerships:** You build strong and trusting relationships both internal and external to the organization.

Take the Quiz

I have turned these five items into a short quiz below. Please rate each indicator (using the definitions above) of organizational resilience based on the following scale:

1. Significant weakness
2. Somewhat weak
3. Neutral
4. Somewhat strong
5. Significant strength

Total your score (the maximum total is 25 points). A higher score is a better result. What are your areas of strength and opportunity? What lessons did you learn from the pandemic? What are you going to do as a first step to address these gaps?

Resilience Indicator	Score
Strong leadership practices	
Motivated workers	
Situational awareness	
Innovation	
Effective partnerships	
	TOTAL:

TNTs to Build Organizational Resilience

Three other suggestions that are critical to organizational resilience, but which may seem counterintuitive, are described below.[168]

TNT: CREATE PRODUCTIVE DISRUPTIONS

When your team or organization is confronting a challenge, it's tempting to meet urgency with speed, but that approach can create dysfunctional momentum. Dysfunctional momentum happens when the team is so focused on action that it fails to notice new problems emerging or changes to the situation. To defeat dysfunctional momentum, create intentional interruptions.[169] Use team huddles to check in with each other about what is truly happening.

TNT: REPURPOSE EXISTING ROUTINES, ROLES, & RESOURCES

Resilient organizations pause first to examine what they have to work with when challenges happen—their routines, roles, and resources. Then they pull pieces of old routines into the new challenge as a formative starting point from which to work.

TNT: TAKE RELATIONAL PAUSES & ADDRESS FRUSTRATION

Emotions generally can get a bad rap at work. It's common for teams to ignore, suppress, or deny emotions, yet negative emotions can fracture teams. To address emotions effectively, take "relational pauses." As a challenge unfolds, teams take time to check in with each other to address how they are all feeling. Relational pauses aren't always easy. They require strong leadership, a team who collectively feels the need to engage this way, empathy, and emotional intelligence.[170] Psychologist Susan David recommends that when you or your team are frustrated and experiencing intense emotions, pause and ask, "What are two other ways to describe how I'm feeling right now?" This question shifts your mindset from stress into one of curiosity, and when you can articulate your stress in a more specific way, you (and others) can better support your teams.

Resilience & Employee Engagement Are Interconnected

Having engaged employees is an important component of resilience. "Work engagement" is defined as having a "positive and fulfilling work-related state of mind" characterized by vigor, dedication, and absorption.[171] What that means is that work engagement requires a blend of energy, mental resilience, recognition and significance, and challenge and growth, and few organizations understand that resilience and engagement are interconnected. Resilience is an important job resource that contributes to higher levels of work engagement, and high levels of work engagement are one of the most important factors to increase organizational resilience.[172] Resilient employees both sustain themselves through challenges and exhibit high levels of self-efficacy (see chapter 4), which lead to enhanced levels of work engagement, suggesting that resilience likely serves to construct a pathway for developing engaged employees.[173] Another study found support for the influence work engagement has on resilience and job performance. What researchers found was that resilience increased job engagement, and those who were more engaged showed higher levels of job performance. Resilience helped workers remain engaged despite the stress they experienced while working.[174] During the pandemic, self-efficacy and having family and friends' support were instrumental in supporting employee resilience, and the resulting resilience was significantly associated with work engagement.[175]

Resilience helps individuals, teams, and organizations better manage the stressors associated with change at work. In addition, building resilience allows teams to pave the way for sustained innovation and growth, proving that adversity is not necessarily a permanent setback but a catalyst for transformative change.

Lead Well: Ideas to Remember

- Resilience at work is a combination of the capacity to navigate problems, obstacles, uncertainties, and challenges and then grow from them. There are important business outcomes associated with resilience.
- Resilient teams do important things before, during, and after both small and large challenges.
- You can use the PRIMED acronym to remember the building blocks of team resilience, and there are four additional capacities to address.
- Resilient teams have good teaming practices and continually ask three important questions: Are we working on the right things? Do we have time to make real progress? Is knowledge easy to find and understand?
- Organizational resilience is created via multiple pathways as well; the five most critical are identified above.
- Your resilience efforts will also reinforce your engagement efforts, and vice versa.

Chapter 7

Mindset #5
Promote Values Alignment & Meaning

A ligned values can lead to greater engagement and autonomy at
work. Nearly one year ago, Natalie Archibald left her dream
job.[176] She led the People team at a large organization, and while she
loved her work, she knew it was time to make her next career move.
The company she worked for had been in hyper-growth mode for
years, and while she was deeply proud of the work she accomplished,
she was also deeply in need of a break. The stress of leading through
a pandemic had taken its toll. Work had become such a large part of
her identity that she didn't even know how to introduce herself without speaking about what she did for a living. When she left, she
knew she was burned out and needed space and time to reset.
Reconnecting with her values energized her and helped her see new
possibilities for her career. Her values of integrity, equality, authen-
ticity, connection, and justice/fairness helped her evolve her leadership style so she could connect with the right type of organization
and make an immediate impact.

Values misalignment was a factor in my own burnout, and now
my core values—kindness and courage—inform every important
decision I make. Kindness comes easily to me; courage does not. But
I know that every single regret I have had in life can be traced back
to failures in one or both of those areas.

Values alignment and having meaningful work are a powerful
one-two punch in the Lead Well framework. Meaning is the subjective experience you have that your work matters, facilitates personal

growth, and is significant and worthwhile.[177] Values are a way of being or believing that you hold most important—they reflect what you care about.[178]

Values misalignment at work occurs when a person's values conflict with their organization's values. That disconnect, over time, is wearing, and values misalignment is one of the Core 6 drivers of chronic stress and disengagement.

Here's what values misalignment sounds like in my workshops:

- When I think about values misalignment, I first think about generational differences. There is a lot of inflexibility around understanding generational differences.
- When my company was acquired, it didn't take long before I noticed a shift from person focus to company focus.
- People around here don't walk the talk—values aren't lived.
- Company values don't often translate into day-to-day practice.
- I want to know how to make an impact and break barriers AND preserve my sanity.
- My wife and I have a two-year-old son, and there is now new management at my wife's company. They are walking back policies, and now it's harder for her to leave work early to pick up our son on time.

Having a clear understanding of your values is a key place to start, and it's also an important aspect of meaningful work. Meaning is powerful workplace psychological fuel. Research has consistently linked meaning at work to dedication to one's career, willingness to put in extra effort into your work role, organizational commitment, and intrinsic work motivation.[179] People who report having meaningful work have lower rates of absenteeism and higher levels of both objective and subjective job performance.[180] One study of more than 20,000 employees across industries found that meaning was a key predictor of workplace thriving (defined as the psychological feeling of both vitality and learning).[181]

However, studies identifying specific leadership practices to foster meaningful work have been limited until now. New research identifies six specific leadership practices that foster meaningful work.[182] One of the things I particularly love about this framework is that it includes values and values alignment within it. In addition, you will notice the prominence of ABC needs.

In the rest of this chapter, I will weave together values and meaning via this new framework. Here are the six practices associated with meaningful work, including case studies, personal stories, and some of my favorite TNTs to help.

Leading for Meaning Practice #1: Communicate the Work's Bigger Impact

The study found that communicating the impact of work was the pathway most strongly associated with meaningful work. People need to feel keenly aware of the connection between their contribution and workplace outcomes. When I interviewed Liz Hall, a former F/A-18 weapons system officer in the Navy, for an article on leadership, she emphasized how important it was to make this connection.[183] She would take extra time to explain a mission in more detail to the person who fueled the aircraft, for example. She showed the approved video sensor footage of a bomb that was dropped to the person who loaded the weapons on the aircraft. Those extra explanations provided inspiration and kept the aircraft maintenance crew involved and feeling like they were connected to the mission and contributing.

TNT: WAYS TO TALK ABOUT IMPACT

Leaders can make these connections for their teams in both formal and informal ways. Here are a few examples:

- Schedule regular meetings with your team to discuss progress on projects and initiatives.

- Quantify work results when you can using data, metrics, and key performance indicators (e.g., our team increases sales by 30% compared to this time last year).
- Celebrate milestones, both big and small. Seeing progress this way, especially in small increments, is critical to motivation, engagement, and also builds self-efficacy.[184]

In addition, values misalignment can happen here when people approach a problem from their own perspective, using their own unique lens (passions, expertise, and responsibilities) to determine what aspects of work are most important, without clarifying how their work fits into the bigger picture.[185] Talking to your team by "speaking" their values back to them can help them better prioritize and feel more connected to their work.

Leading for Meaning Practice #2: Recognize & Nurture Potential

This pathway showed the second strongest correlation with meaningful work. It's important for busy professionals to feel effective at work and be challenged (the "C" of the ABC needs). High-performing teams, at their core, are about solving hard problems together. To do that effectively and to feel like you're growing and developing at work, you must set sticky goals.

TNT: SET STICKY GOALS

Improving performance and enhancing your skills starts with a goal. What do you want to accomplish or improve? You and your team need to take a realistic approach to successfully arrive at a given outcome. You can do this by going through a process called mental contrasting.[186] The questions I have included in Steps 1–3 below come from a powerful process called appreciative inquiry. Appreciative inquiry's assumption is simple: "Every [team] has something that works well, and those strengths can be the starting point for creating positive change and/or a positive future."[187] There are four steps to the process:

- **Step 1:** Identify a goal or an outcome you want to achieve.
  - ◦ What matters most to you or your team?
  - ◦ What would the future of your team (or the future generally) look like if you consistently had the best examples happening at work?
- **Step 2:** List specific pathways that will help you accomplish this goal.
  - ◦ What are the pathways that will take you from where you are now to the future you're hoping to create?
- **Step 3:** List the obstacles that may get in your way.
  - ◦ What obstacles/barriers exist?
- **Step 4:** Create your plan, also called your implementation intention.
  - ◦ Research shows that one of the ways to make your plan "stick" is to build in implementation intentions. Implementation intentions are a way for you to plan in advance how to deal with the obstacles that arise.[188] One highly effective type of implementation intention is "if-then" planning: If X happens, then I will do Y.[189]

Table 7.1 is an example of how I've used this process.

Leading for Meaning Practice #3: Foster Personal Connections

I talked about the importance of workplace connection and friendships in chapter 4 (the "B" of the ABC needs), and it also made me think of my work with the military, where I first learned of a concept called "battle buddies." A battle buddy is someone a solider can rely on, someone who is there for support and accountability as

Table 7.1. My Sticky Goals Analysis

My goal: I want to spend more quality time with my eight-year-old daughter, Lucy.

Pathways	Obstacles
• Leave work early two nights/week. • Read more books with her at night. • Plan a long weekend getaway. • On her next day off of school, take the day off instead of sending her to school camp. • Volunteer together.	• My travel schedule • Running out of time at night doing other things/eating/basic evening chores • Writing this book • Solo parenting • Running a growing business

Plan/Implementation Intention: If there is a month when I know I will be traveling a lot, then I will plan to pick Lucy up as soon as school ends, at least three times that month to have fun and hang out. One of the reasons why this helps so much is that I can now scan my calendar months in advance and orient my time much more intentionally when I know I have a lot of travel scheduled.

needed, someone who can motivate you when you're down and help you manage tough times but who lives in the same "world" that you do and is at about your same level.[190] Who is that person or who are those people for you?

One interesting study examined the relationship between peer support and competency exam performance among physicians.[191] The study looked at a cohort of surgeons, specifically, and found that those solo practitioners who had fewer routine peer interactions had worse exam performance (exam scores were 2 percentage points lower than physicians practicing in groups, and 4.5% of the solo practitioners failed the exam compared to 0.9% of surgeons in group practice). The level of peer interaction explained the relationship between solo practice and poor exam performance. However, solo practitioners who reported more frequent peer interactions had scores as high as the physicians in group practice. The study concluded that interactions with peers were a critical part of professional learning and development, suggesting that professionals need to be connected to colleagues through a variety of learning initiatives like conferences, professional networks, and day-to-day interaction.

Reviving dormant connections is a powerful way to increase connection.

TNT: REVIVE DORMANT CONNECTIONS

Your network is composed of three types of connections or ties: strong ties, dormant ties, and weak ties. When you need advice or help, whether it be personal or professional, most people rely on their strong ties. What many of us miss, though, is how powerful reconnecting with our dormant connections might be. A dormant connection is a person you haven't been in touch with for at least three years; a connection that has gone quiet but was likely strong to begin with. Dormant connections introduce a diverse network of people and ideas that might be as valuable (or more so) than your strong connections.

Here's the catch. Very few people want to be the one to initiate contact with someone they've lost touch with. In a series of studies, researchers found that most people (90%) had lost touch with a friend but expressed little interest in reconnecting.[192] Even more interesting, fewer than one-third of the study participants sent a message to an old friend, even when they wanted to, thought the friend would be appreciative, had the friend's contact information, and were given time to draft and send a message! Why? The top three reasons were (1) the friend might not be interested in hearing from me (which is an odd reason considering that most of them said they thought the friend would react positively); (2) that it would be awkward after all this time; and (3) they didn't want to bother the person. The only thing that helped the study participants actually take action and reach out was the activity the researchers asked the participants to perform. First, they were told to spend three minutes sending messages to several *current* friends or acquaintances. Then, participants were encouraged to send a message to their dormant connection and were told that it was an act of kindness that would be appreciated by the dormant connection. The act of sending messages to current friends made the participants more likely to send messages to old ones; in fact, this one activity increased the number of people who reached out to an old friend by two-thirds. So, if you're stuck wanting to reach out to an old friend or contact, start by sending a few messages to current ones to get you going.

Personally, I have experienced the power of revived dormant connections very recently. My college roommate, Katrina, reached out to tell me that her mom was sick. I was so happy to hear from her (though not about that news), and we texted back and forth for a while. Then she asked, "Can I call you?" I said of course, and we talked for almost an hour. I had tears hearing that familiar, sweet voice from so long ago. We decided to create a group text chat that included our other college roommates, which has been fun. I now have a new source of reconnection (and an outlet for support), and it makes me so happy.

The pandemic made relationships challenging in so many ways. Who will you reconnect with?

Leading for Meaning Practice #4: Discuss Values & Purpose during Hiring and Onboarding

As the pandemic began to ease, I worked with a team that is part of a large employment website for job listings. Sixty-six members of the team took an assessment to better understand the root causes of their high stress and burnout. Unmanageable workload was the main driver of stress, and the senior leadership team was not surprised by this finding. What was surprising, though, was the ambivalence related to some of the statements about recognition practices, strength of community, and fairness, with many marking statements "hard to decide." If policies are fair, if you feel appreciated, and if you feel connected to your team, you wouldn't answer "hard to decide." When I talked to the leadership team about some of these responses, they mentioned that more than half of their team had just joined the organization in the several months prior to the assessment. That is likely a strong reason why a respondent might score "hard to decide" to a statement—they simply don't know the team culture well enough yet.

It also underscores, though, the work that organizations, leaders, and teams need to do to make sure people feel appreciated, policies are clear, core values are discussed, and efforts are made to connect people to their teams and to the organization immediately. Fostering strong alignment between a person and his or her work begins at onboarding.

It's been a while since I've worked in a traditional job, but I remember onboarding as an endless parade of benefits forms, rules, and documents to read. Many organizations miss this prime opportunity to connect new hires with the mission and values of the business.

TNT: 3 FACTORS THAT SUPPORT POSITIVE ONBOARDING

Is there an ideal way to onboard new employees in the era of hybrid work? The answer is "yes." Researchers at Microsoft have studied thriving, which they define as being energized and empowered to do meaningful work. They wanted to see whether there was an ideal way to onboard new employees, particularly in a way that would promote thriving for the new employee. Tailored approaches can be beneficial, but these were the top three factors that made the most difference:[193]

1. Clarity about role responsibilities
2. Feedback on how the new hire is doing
3. Resources to help them answer questions

As you think about how your employees are onboarded, are these practices being incorporated? In addition, leaders would be wise to make note of those on their team who were hired during the pandemic to make sure they retroactively receive the same standard and level of onboarding that in-office or hybrid employees currently do.[194]

TNT: ASSIGN AN ONBOARDING PARTNER

Another idea leaders should consider is assigning an onboarding partner to a new hire.[195] The onboarding partner can be responsible for making sure the three factors above actually happen, and they can help connect new employees with potential mentors, coaches, and peers, thus helping them develop clear networks that are also so critical to connecting, particularly in a distributed workplace.

Leading for Meaning Practice #5: Model Values-Based Behavior

It's important for workers to see leaders walk the talk—acting and leading in alignment with stated organizational values. This practice was the most negatively correlated with low intention to leave, meaning that when employees see their leaders acting in a way that is contrary to values-based behaviors, they may be more likely to leave.[196]

The leaders I interviewed for this book all had one thing in common: their commitment and connection to both personal and organizational values. As you have read, many of them had to make critical decisions about direction, personnel, and other matters, and they leaned into their values when doing so.

You can learn more about what your team values by going through the exercise below.

TNT: CREATE A BIGGER-THAN-TEAM GOAL

While this strategy has been written about with an individual focus, I have adapted it to help your team think about identifying and applying its values at work.[197] Consider the following questions:

1. What is the positive impact your team wants to have in the organization? Within the division or larger work unit?
2. What are your team's values and how are they lived?
3. What type of positive change do you want to make or create within the organization, division, or larger work unit?
4. What would your clients, customers, or patients say about how your team helps them?

5. How does your team support the greater mission of the organization?

Any one of these questions alone would be a wonderful entry point to collect stories from your team about what they value about their work. You will likely uncover stories that you may have never heard that can be shared with the organization at large or otherwise promoted (or even shared with new employees as part of the onboarding process). Storytelling is a phenomenal way to promote values.

You should also take some time to discuss what forces pull you away from those values. Is it too many competing priorities? Did a close work colleague leave, removing a key relationship and source of connection for you and/or the team? Something else?

Leading for Meaning Practice #6: Give Employees Autonomy

I discussed autonomy at length in chapter 4 (the "A" of the ABC needs). Here are some additional TNTs to boost autonomy.

TNT: THE 4/4/4 WAY TO END YOUR WEEK

An important way for leaders to foster autonomy is to support a bottom-up approach to work design. Job crafting helps people take a more personalized approach to their work by taking control and shifting aspects of their work (their tasks, how they interact with others, how they think about the value and significance of their work, how they pursue knowledge and learning opportunities, and what promotes well-being) in subtle ways to better align their work with their personal needs, skills, and interests.[198] Research has consistently linked job crafting to higher levels of overall job engagement and job satisfaction, to higher quality of care in hospitals and nursing homes, to innovation and creativity, and to reduced levels of burnout, depression, and job strain.[199]

While there are lots of ways to enable employees to "micro-craft" aspects of their job by making small changes or creating new habits,

I want to focus in one area and on one skill that is powerful. I call it the 4/4/4 way to end your week. Each "4" represents an activity that you can do in four minutes of time, for a total of 12 minutes. I thought 12 minutes was a doable amount of time for anybody, regardless of title and level of busyness. First, I want you to set a reminder in your calendar to try this process on whatever day you consider to be the end of your week. I'm going to suggest Friday. Then, follow these steps (which leverage an important trio of activities to savor, reflect, and capitalize on positive workplace experiences):

- **Step 1:** Spend four minutes thinking about and/or writing down the positive experiences you had during your week at work. How did you make progress in your work, even if that progress was small? What role did you play in bringing about the good result?
- **Step 2:** Spend four minutes thinking about what you want to focus on in the coming week; specifically, thinking in terms of the tasks you want to start or complete, relationships you want to strengthen, and personal strengths and values you want to exhibit or bring more fully into alignment.
- **Step 3:** Spend four minutes sending a note of appreciation, recognition, or gratitude to someone (or more than one person). Be specific in your note by using the thank you "plus" phrasing you learned about in chapter 3. If you can, try to share this sentiment either in person, by phone, or by live virtual connection such as Zoom or Microsoft Teams.

This exercise combines several research strands that taken together create a large autonomy and well-being boost. First, one of the single biggest things you and your team can do to create energy, motivation, and positive emotions is to talk about work progress.[200] Second, employees can increase the benefits of positive workplace experiences by savoring them.[201] Finally, the well-being outcomes associated with this process include more positive emotions, higher work engagement, better sleep quality, reduced fatigue and burnout, and lower stress.[202]

TNT: USE THE 20% RULE

Another way for leaders and teams to micro-craft aspects of their job is to use the 20% rule. Take a moment and list the specific aspects of your work that you find most meaningful. A physician might list patient care, research, educating future doctors, and/or making scientific discoveries. A salesperson might list following up with clients, learning new aspects of a product to sell, or preparing new quotes and proposals. Then estimate the percentage of time you spend in each of those areas.

Is there a disconnect between what you listed as meaningful and how much time you spend in that area? For many people, the answer is "yes." Interestingly, one study found that professionals who spent less than 20% of their time on their most meaningful aspect of work had almost double the rate of burnout as their colleagues who spent closer to 20% of their time focused on a meaningful area.[203]

As we have already discussed, unmanageable workloads, unclear expectations, and too many meetings are just a few of the things that can pull your people away from implementing the 20% rule. Some people find that to get close to 20%, they need to make micro-changes in the way they work. These micro-changes might involve blocking off specific chunks of time on your calendar or reordering your day to prioritize your most meaningful tasks when you know you're most likely to do them.[204]

TNT: TRY THE 3-3-3 TIME METHOD

Another strategy to help you implement the 20% rule or to simply help you keep some order and control to your day is the 3-3-3 method that Oliver Burkeman writes about in his book *Four Thousand Weeks*. According to this method, you should aim for the following each day:[205]

- **3 hours:** Spend three hours on your most important current project, making sure to do this creative, deep thinking during the span of time when your energy is the highest.

- **3 shorter tasks:** Complete three shorter tasks, such as urgent to-do's, making calls, attending meetings.
- **3 maintenance activities:** Complete three healthy habits and/or daily administrative tasks, such as a break to talk to a friend or starting the morning with some exercise.

These six leadership practices have been found to strongly correlate with mattering (chapter 3), intrinsic work motivation (chapter 4), and job satisfaction.[206] This means that certain of these strategies can do double or triple duty—building meaning, mattering, and intrinsic work motivation.

My mentor, Dr. Shane Lopez, said it best: "Followers look to leaders to capitalize on the spirit and ideas of the times, to dream big, and to motivate them toward a meaningful future." That spirit is needed now more than ever.

Lead Well: Ideas to Remember

- Employees crave meaning and values alignment in their work experiences. Values misalignment is a Core 6 factor that drives chronic stress and burnout at work.
- There are six leadership practices to help your team build meaning at work, and three of those practices overlap with the ABC needs outlined in chapter 4.
- Speaking in the language of an employee's values can help them to prioritize their work and more clearly see the impact they are making.
- There are ways you can "micro-craft" your work—shifting aspects of your work in subtle ways to better align with your strengths, goals, and values.

Conclusion
Implementing the Lead Well Mindsets

For teams to thrive today and in the future, leaders need new mindsets that will help engage, retain, and inspire their teams. They need to see the people side of their work as equally important to the performance side—as a leadership competency to develop. Specifically, leaders need to think about the drivers of engagement, retention, flexibility, community, and purpose, knowing that old ways of thinking won't lead to the future state of collective thriving that is desired. The Lead Well mindsets presented in this book will be a source of resilience, stability, and future growth for your teams and organizations. These mindsets will help you create a teaming environment that leads to more meaning, mattering, flexibility, engagement, thriving, and stronger relationships—the type of culture we all want at work.

But, there's something I want to acknowledge in this conclusion, and it's been on my mind as I've been writing this book. It's quite likely that you're also overwhelmed, tired, and maybe even feeling burned out. Managers and leaders across levels are burning out and leaving their jobs at an alarming rate. Managers are more likely than nonmanagers to be disengaged at work, burned out, looking for a new job, and feeling like their organization doesn't care about their well-being.[207] More than a quarter of leaders in 2024 feel burned out often or always, and two-thirds feel it at least sometimes.[208] More than 1,400 CEOs left their jobs between January and September 2023, an increase of almost 50% compared to 2022, and it's the biggest turnover at that level in more than two decades.[209] In addition, 71% of the C-suite reported that they are seriously contemplating quitting their jobs for one that better supports their well-being, and 66% of managers said the same thing.[210]

Companies are ready to find new leaders who are prepared to address how the world has changed and the ongoing volatile business landscape. Some of it is burnout—the pandemic put a huge amount of pressure on CEOs and leaders to navigate unprecedented challenges under increased scrutiny from almost all of their constituencies. Further, many leaders I talk to report that they take on their employees' extra work so as not to burn them out. They are falling on their own burnout sword to save their teams, and none of this is helpful. Managers have more work, fewer people (or newer teams), and tighter budgets. That's a tough gauntlet to ride.

That's why I made the Lead Well mindsets simple to execute. There is a lot of information contained in each mindset, but I hope you see how important it is to look at issues of well-being from a root-cause systemic approach. And you now know there is a true positive business case associated with doing so. Creating a thriving team culture is a team sport that you lead. You don't have to (and shouldn't) do it all by yourself. Many of the practices I shared will be ones you can do together with your team, or you may even use them for yourself or suggest what would be good for individuals on your team to try too.

Here's a process that I hope will make the Lead Well mindsets as easy to implement as possible:

1. **Remember the Core 6 and the ABCs.** If you do nothing else, I want you to more consistently think about and discuss the Core 6 and the ABCs. I created downloads for each of these frameworks. They can be found via the link referenced in the "Resource Center" section below.

2. **Identify the biggest challenge and map it to the most relevant mindset.** Ask, "What is our biggest area of concern right now?" Is it lack of community due to hybrid work and/or

return to office policies? If so, then look at the ways to foster belonging and connection (the "B" of the ABC needs) in chapter 4 or via meaningful work in chapter 7. Is it unmanageable workload? Skip to chapter 5. Do you know that you need to improve recognition practices? Then start with chapter 3.

3. **Ask, "What support do I need?"** These strategies take self-awareness, practice, and time to turn into habits. Not all leaders are used to thinking about the psychology of thriving and great teamwork, so this may feel new to you. Do you need:

- Coaching to help put the skills into practice in a more specific way that matches your day-to-day challenges and to strategize about next steps?
- Guides, worksheets, and templates to help transfer the knowledge and for use with your team?
- Suggestions for assessment tools to measure progress?
- Support from internal or external resources, or both?
- Leader cover and support?
- Periodic reminders?

TNT: CHANGE YOUR PASSWORDS

I want to share with you one last TNT, and it's one of my secrets to helping people make something a habit. I want you to change your password to reflect a value, goal, or positive emotion you want to work toward, and it can be related or unrelated to the Lead Well mindsets. I started talking about this technique after I read an article about a guy who wanted to forgive his wife after their divorce. He changed his password to "forgive@her," and he found it so helpful that he used the technique again to stop smoking. This works because it's a form of priming—helping to activate nonconscious processes (processes that do not require conscious control) to facilitate goal achievement and self-regulation.[211]

I'm not a fan of setting New Year's resolutions; instead, I create a "word of the year." I choose one word that I want to govern my decisions, my time, and my behavior during the upcoming year. Then I modify my passwords accordingly so that I'm intentionally keeping that word front of mind multiple times each day.

Here are some examples of how my clients and others have used this technique:

- My friend changed her password to "gratitude." Not long after she did this, she lost her job. She said it helped her deal with the negative emotions and other psychological fallout because the password reminder helped her to think of instances of gratitude multiple times each day.
- A client said she changed her password to "appreciate@kelly" because Kelly was a valuable member of her team. My client realized that her perfectionistic tendencies were causing other valued members of her team to leave, and she wanted to make sure Kelly stayed.

Resource Center

I have created templates and worksheets for many of the TNTs I explain in this book. You can access the TNTs, as well as the following, on my website, www.stressandresilience.com:

- **Summary of skills:** I have created a Lead Well Summary that sorts the different TNTs, by chapter, into one document.
- **Bonus chapter:** You can download a bonus chapter I wrote that specifically addresses leader burnout. I want you to feel like you can Lead Well and perform at your best, given all the stress and pressure you face.

A Great Culture Just Feels Good

I want to share with you one final story. On the Smuggler's Notch side of the Green Mountains in Vermont, you will find Becca and Doug Worple, owners of the Golden Dog Farm in Jeffersonville. My daughter Lucy and I recently visited the farm, and for almost two hours on two separate days in July, Lucy and I played with about a dozen golden retrievers. We had the time of our lives, and it's one of the best things she and I have done together. We met people of all ages, from all over the country, who, like us, made their way to a tiny town in Vermont to play with a bunch of dogs. It was the golden retriever version of *Field of Dreams*.

At the end of the second day of our visit, I talked to Becca, as I was curious to know more about how she and her husband ended up in Vermont producing honey, maple syrup, wine, and, well, playing with dogs.[212] She told me that they worked for many years in a variety of "corporate" jobs. Doug eventually landed a senior role at a global digital advertising agency, which required extensive travel. When the pandemic started, Doug's travel stopped and, like many others, they used it as an opportunity to consider what was next. They sold their house intending to drive to a family cottage in Ottawa, Canada, but the border closed. As Plan B, they decided to rent an apartment in Cincinnati, where they lived, but at the last minute the landlord backed out of the lease. They were now without a home, and as Plan C they decided to buy an RV and drive around the United States to find their next thing. Thirty-five states and 17,000 miles later, they ended up in Jeffersonville, Vermont, where they spotted Dana Menne driving around town with a truck full of golden retrievers. Doug and Becca owned goldens at the time and took it as a sign that they had found their forever home. The couple purchased a farm outside of town and partnered with Dana and his wife Susan, who are golden retriever breeders, to start the Golden Retriever Experience in September 2023.

What has stayed with me about our visit is the power and intensity of the emotions that I experienced and saw others experience while we were there. I have asked myself why watching other people be so excited and happy about being with a few dogs made me so emotional—like tears in my eyes happy because they were so happy. And what surprised me was how few kids were there. I expected the experience to be predominantly young kids and families, and that wasn't the case. In fact, Lucy was the only child there on our second day at the farm. It was mostly adults who wanted a chance to feel like kids again. To experience a level of joy that has been missing.

While I think that having a "happy" (the collective noun they coined for a group of goldens) of goldens at your disposal would solve a lot of workplace angst, I know it's more of a far-fetched idea (pun intended) than reality. What makes people feel like they're running with a happy of goldens is being able to answer "yes" to these questions:[213]

- Am I energized by my work/work environment?
- Can I navigate uncertainty, challenge, and setback—and grow from it?
- Do I have opportunities to learn and grow?
- Do I matter and does my work matter?

The Lead Well mindsets will help you answer these questions and do so much more for the health and well-being of your team. You've got this!

Acknowledgments

We can only be said to be alive in those moments when our hearts are conscious of our treasures.
—Thornton Wilder

Writing a book is an all-consuming process. When you say yes to a commitment like this one, everyone in your life comes along for the ride. Writing this book became the primary focus of my work—and a huge focus of my life. The words, ideas, and stories became a friend, of sorts, that never left my side for more than a year. I simply could not have finished it without a tremendous amount of help, love, and support. I am deeply grateful to everyone who helped put this book's message into the world.

A huge thank you to my clients. You gave me a front-row seat to your struggles and triumphs, and you helped me understand what it means to Lead Well. Thank you so much for sharing your stories, both publicly for this book and privately. It has been an honor to help you do the great work you do, and this book exists because of your wisdom.

Thank you to my editors past and present at *Forbes*, *Fast Company*, and *Psychology Today* for giving me a platform to find my voice, raise awareness, teach others, evolve my thinking, and talk openly about the stressors associated with work and life.

I have a fantastic team! Thank you to Megan Thompson, Nancy Sheed, Anne Allen, Patrick Powers, the team at Target Marketing, and the team at Cave Henricks Communications. Thank you for keeping my head above water and helping me continue to grow my business.

This book would not have happened without Shannon Berning at Wharton School Press. I emailed her last year to let her know that I had an idea for a second book. It took me three tries before I finally decided to write what was in my heart, and she patiently let that process unfold. Thank you also to the rest of the team at Wharton School Press: I truly value our partnership. And of course, thank you to my agent, Ivor Whitson, who took a chance on me many years ago and always believed there was a place in the world for my books.

My life changed significantly in the past few years. I would not have made it through without the love and support of my friends: my chosen family. They have held my hand, listened, wiped my tears, celebrated life, encouraged, inspired, and asked me the tough questions when I most needed to hear them. Thank you, Julie Miller, Wendy Althen, Kim VanVoorhees Bell, Tasha Bernard, Pamela Peterson Coviello, David Austin, Dan Mason, Justin Daniels, Brent Sicely, and Sylvia Lopez. I'm so thankful to have reconnected with my girls from Trowbridge Hall: Katrina Gustum Chovan, Sharon Laatsch, Kristi Dobson, Joy Randle Mankel, and Brenda Peters-Grass.

A special thank you to my neighbors, Sarah Remmel and Peter McCauley. Thank you for watching Lucy when I needed a run, to finish some work, or to run a few errands. Thank you also for getting my mail and watching the house when I travel. It makes leaving town a bit more peaceful knowing I don't have to worry about anything. We need a special Eddie's dinner to celebrate this one!

To my parents, Bob and Trish Davis. I'm so glad more people will know about the business you created, which inspired my own entrepreneurial journey. You are both fantastic role models. Thank you for all the business and life advice, and for watching Lucy so I could work on this book. To my brother Jeff, sister-in-law Cortney, and nephew Owen: Lucy and I miss you all so much from across the ocean.

Tom: You get an extra big thank you. You've been through this process before, and you know the level of commitment involved. Thank you for watching Lucy on too many weekends to count so I could focus on writing.

And finally, to my dear daughter, Lucy Tess. Out of the billions of people on the planet, we somehow found each other. I love watching you grow into your kindness, confidence, and determination. You have already influenced more lives than you know. Being your mom is my greatest joy, and as I tell you every night at bed: Out of all the babies in the whole world, I got the best one.

Notes

Introduction

1 Interview with Robert & Patricia Davis, September 5, 2024.

2 Christine Ipsen, Maria Karanika-Murray, & Giulia Nardelli (2020). Addressing Mental Health and Organizational Performance in Tandem: A Challenge and an Opportunity for Bringing Together What Belongs Together. 34(1) *Work & Stress*, 1–4.

3 Richard G. Tedeschi & Lawrence G. Calhoun (2004). Posttraumatic Growth: Conceptual Foundations & Empirical Evidence. 15(1) *Psychological Inquiry*, 1–18.

4 Aaron DeSmet, Arne Gast, Johanne Lavoie, & Michael Lurie (May 4, 2023). New Leadership for a New Era of Thriving Organizations. McKinsey & Company. https://www.mckinsey.com/capabilities/people-and-organizational -performance/our-insights/new-leadership-for-a-new-era-of-thriving -organizations.

5 David Green (December 2023). 12 Opportunities for HR in 2024: From Support Function to Strategic Partner. *Data Driven HR Monthly Newsletter*. LinkedIn. https://www.linkedin.com/pulse/12-opportunities-hr-2024-from-support-function -david-green--rsq3e/?trackingId=SqV%2BR1jbQlaDNICCbVl7sg%3D%3D.

6 Chelsea LeNoble, Anthony Naranjo, Mindy Shoss, & Kristin Horan (2023). Navigating a Context of Severe Uncertainty: The Effect of Industry Unsafety Signals on Employee Well-Being During the COVID-19 Crisis. 7 *Occupational Health Science*, 707–743.

7 Anna Medaris (January–February 2024). People Want Meaning and Stability in Their Work. *Monitor on Psychology: 12 Emerging Trends for 2024*. American Psychological Association, 64–67.

8 David Mallon et al. (2024). What Do Organizations Need Most in a Disrupted, Boundaryless Age? More Imagination. In *2024 Global Human Trends Report*. Deloitte, 52–65. https://www2.deloitte.com/content/dam/insights/articles /glob176836_global-human-capital-trends-2024/DI_Global-Human-Capital -Trends-2024.pdf.

9 YMCA WorkWell (2022). *Insights to Impact: Hope & Renewal: Small Steps Toward Healthier Workplaces*. https://www.ymcaworkwell.com/insights-to -impact-2022.

10 Medaris (2024), 67.

Chapter 1

11 Interview with Jay Shah, July 1, 2024.

12 Alex Camp, Arne Gast, Drew Goldstein, & Brooke Weddle (February 12, 2024). Organizational Health Is (Still) the Key to Long-Term Performance. McKinsey & Company. https://www.mckinsey.com/capabilities/people-and-organizational -performance/our-insights/organizational-health-is-still-the-key-to-long-term -performance.

13 Susan Lund et al. (February 18, 2021). *The Future of Work After COVID-19.* McKinsey Global Institute, https://www.mckinsey.com/featured-insights/future -of-work/the-future-of-work-after-covid-19.

14 The Future of the Great Resignation: What Employers Need to Know for 2023. Indeed. https://www.indeed.com/hire/c/info/future-of-the-great-resignation.

15 Huileng Tan (January 19, 2023). More Than Half of US Workers Want to Quit Their Jobs in 2023, a New Survey Shows. *Business Insider.* https://www.businessinsider .com/great-resignation-linkedin-us-workers-considering-quitting-2023-1.

16 Tan (2023).

17 PwC (2022). *Global Workforce Hope & Fears Survey 2022.* https://www.pwc.com /gx/en/hopes-and-fears/downloads/global-workforce-hopes-and-fears-survey -2022-v2.pdf.

18 PwC (2022).

19 Ben Wigert & Ryan Pendell (January 31, 2023). Six Trends Leaders Need to Navigate This Year. Gallup. https://www.gallup.com/workplace/468173 /workplace-findings-leaders-need-navigate-year.aspx.

20 Ben Wigert (December 18, 2023). Six Workplace Trends Leaders Should Watch in 2024. Gallup. https://www.gallup.com/workplace/547283/workplace-trends -leaders-watch-2024.aspx.

21 Interview with Jen Fisher, February 10, 2024.

22 Interview with Marti Wronski, August 5, 2024.

23 Lund et al. (February 18, 2021). See also, Gabriella Rosen Kellerman & Martin Seligman (2023). *Tomorrowmind: Thriving at Work with Resilience, Creativity, and Connection—Now and in an Uncertain Future.* New York: Atria Books.

24 Kellerman & Seligman (2023), 222.

25 Gallup (2024). *State of the Global Workplace 2024.* https://www.gallup.com /workplace/349484/state-of-the-global-workplace.aspx.

26 Gallup (2024).

27 Jen Fisher, Sue Cantrell, Jay Bhatt, & Paul H. Silverglate (June 18, 2024). The Important Role of Leaders in Advancing Human Sustainability. https://www2 .deloitte.com/us/en/insights/topics/talent/workplace-well-being-research-2024 .html. (Reporting on findings from Deloitte's third *Workplace Well-Being* report.)

28 Jacqueline Brassey et al. (May 27, 2022). Addressing Employee Burnout: Are You Solving the Right Problem? McKinsey Health Institute. https://www.mckinsey .com/~/media/mckinsey/mckinsey%20health%20institute/our%20insights /addressing%20employee%20burnout%20are%20you%20solving%20the%20 right%20problem/addressing-employee-burnout-are-you-solving-the-right -problem-vf.pdf?shouldIndex=false.

29 Amaia Noguera Lasa, Andrea Pedroni, & Asmus Komm (with Simon Gallot Lavallee) (May 15, 2024). In the Spotlight: Performance Management That Puts People First. McKinsey & Company. https://www.mckinsey.com/capabilities /people-and-organizational-performance/our-insights/in-the-spotlight -performance-management-that-puts-people-first#/.

30 Fisher et al. (2024).

31 Workforce Institute at UKG (2023). *Mental Health at Work: Managers and Money.* https://www.ukg.com/resources/white-paper/mental-health-work -managers-and-money.

32 Jan Luca Pletzer, Kimberley Breevaart, & Arnold B. Bakker (2023). Constructive and Destructive Leadership in Job Demands-Resources Theory: A Meta-Analytic Test of the Motivational and Health-Impairment Pathways. *Organizational Psychology Review*, 1–35.

33 Jim Clifton & Jim Harter (2023). *Culture Shock.* Washington, DC: Gallup Press.

34 Jen Fisher, Paul H. Silverglate, Colleen Bordeaux, & Michael Gilmartin (June 20, 2023). As Workforce Well-Being Dips, Leaders Ask: What Will It Take to Move the Needle? Deloitte. https://www2.deloitte.com/us/en/insights/topics/talent /workplace-well-being-research.html.

35 Fisher et al. (2023).

36 Clifton & Harter (2023).

37 Clifton & Harter (2023), 142.

38 Bastiaan Starink & Jan Willem Velthuijsen (May 2022). The Benefits of Investing in People: Where Should Companies Invest to Improve the Employee Experience? PwC. https://www.pwc.nl/en/insights-and-publications/services -and-industries/people-and-organisation/investment-in-employee-experience -reduces-absenteeism-and-turnover.html.

39 Tait Shanafelt, Joel Goh, & Christine Sinsky (2017). The Business Case for Investing in Physician Well-Being. 177(12) *JAMA Internal Medicine*, 1826–1832.

40 Jan-Emmanuel De Neve, Micah Kaats, & George Ward (2023). Workplace Wellbeing and Firm Performance. University of Oxford Well-Being Research Center Working Paper 2304.

41 De Neve et al. (2023), 29.

42 De Neve et al. (2023), 4.

43 De Neve et al. (2023), 21–27.

44 Anu Madgavkar et al. (2023). *Performance Through People: Transforming Human Capital into Competitive Advantage.* McKinsey Global Institute. https://www.mckinsey.com/~/media/mckinsey/mckinsey%20global%20institute /our%20research/performance%20through%20people%20transforming%20 human%20capital%20into%20competitive%20advantage/mgi-performance -through-people-full-report-vf.pdf.

45 Madgavkar et al. (2023), v.

46 Madgavkar et al. (2023), 22.

Chapter 2

47 Brassey et al. (2022).

48 Mallon et al. (2024), 59.

49 Christina Maslach (1998). A Multi-Dimensional Theory of Burnout. In *Theories of Organizational Stress* (Cary L. Cooper, ed.), 68–85. Oxford: Oxford University Press; Christina Maslach, Wilmar B. Schaufeli, & Michael P. Leiter (2001). Job Burnout. 52 *Annual Review of Psychology*, 397–422; Christina Maslach & Michael P. Leiter (2008). Early Predictors of Job Burnout & Engagement. 93 *Journal of Applied Psychology*, 498–512; Omer Aydemir & Ilkin Icelli (2013). *Burnout: Risk Factors.* In *Burnout for Experts: Prevention in the Context of Living and Working* (Sabine Bahrer-Kohler, ed.), 119–143. New York: Springer; Christina Maslach & Michael P. Leiter (2022). *The Burnout Challenge: Managing People's Relationships with Their Jobs.* Cambridge, MA: Harvard University Press.

50 Edward L. Deci & Richard M. Ryan (2014). The Importance of Universal Psychological Needs for Understanding Motivation in the Workplace. In *The Oxford Handbook of Work Engagement, Motivation and Self-Determination Theory* (Marylène Gagné, ed.), 13–32. New York: Oxford University Press.

51 Edward L. Deci & Richard M. Ryan (2000). The "What" and "Why" of Goal Pursuits: Human Needs and the Self-Determination of Behavior. 11(4) *Psychological Inquiry*, 227–268. See also Maarten Vansteenkiste, Richard M. Ryan, & Bart Soenens (2020). Basic Psychological Need Theory: Advancements, Critical Themes, and Future Directions. 44 *Motivation and Emotions*, 1–31.

52 Office of the Surgeon General (2022). *The U.S. Surgeon General's Framework for Workplace Mental Health & Well-Being.* Washington, DC: Department of Health and Human Services.

53 National Academy of Medicine (2019). *Taking Action Against Clinician Burnout: A Systems Approach to Professional Well-Being.* Washington, DC: National Academies Press.

54 Aaron DeSmet, Marino Mugayar-Baldocchi, Angelika Reich, & Bill Schaninger (September 11, 2023). Some Employees Are Destroying Value. Others Are Building It. Do You Know the Difference? McKinsey & Company. https://www

.mckinsey.com/capabilities/people-and-organizational-performance/our
-insights/some-employees-are-destroying-value-others-are-building-it-do-you
-know-the-difference.

55 Zachary A. Mercurio, Tamara Myles, Wesley Adams, & Jeremy D. Clifton
    (2024). Mapping and Measuring Leadership Practices Intended to Foster
    Meaningful Work. 8 *Occupational Health Science*, 435–469.

56 Jari J. Hakanen, Arnold B. Bakker, & Jarno Turunen (2024). The Relative
    Importance of Various Job Resources for Work Engagement: A Concurrent and
    Follow-Up Dominance Analysis. 27(3) *Business Research Quarterly*, 227–243.

57 Hakanen, Bakker, & Turunen (2024).

58 Jan Luca Pletzer, Kimberley Breevaart, & Arnold B. Bakker (2024). Constructive
    and Destructive Leadership in Job Demands-Resources Theory: A Meta-
    Analytic Test of the Motivational and Health-Impairment Pathways. 14(1)
    Organizational Psychology Review, 131–165.

59 Some of the ideas in this section come from Seligman & Kellerman (2023),
    208–219.

60 Seligman & Kellerman (2023), 211.

61 Interview with Wronski.

62 Starink & Velthuijsen (2022); Seligman & Kellerman (2023).

Chapter 3

63 I first learned about Rahan Staton and his mission from a *CBS Mornings*
    interview. You can read more about that interview here: Steve Hartman (May 26,
    2023). A Former Sanitation Worker Just Graduated from Harvard, but Doesn't
    Forget Where He Came From. CBS News. https://www.cbsnews.com/news
    /rehan-staton-sanitation-worker-harvard-law-school-graduate-honors
    -custodians-support-staff/. You can learn more about his nonprofit, The
    Reciprocity Effect, at www.thereciprocityeffect.org.

64 Noguera Lasa et al. (2024).

65 Interview with Jason Zachariah, February 12, 2024.

66 Roy Saunderson (2016). Employee Recognition: Perspectives from the
    Field. In *The Psychologically Healthy Workplace: Building a Win-Win
    Environment for Organizations and Employees* (Matthew J. Grawitch &
    David W. Ballard, eds.), 181–198. Washington, DC: American Psychological
    Association.

67 Jay Bhatt, Colleen Bordeaux, & Jen Fisher (March 13, 2023). The Workforce
    Well-Being Imperative: Paving the Way for Human Sustainability in Workplace
    Culture. Deloitte. https://www2.deloitte.com/us/en/insights/topics/talent
    /employee-wellbeing.html.

68   Paula Davis & American Law Media (2023). The Impact of Stress on Lawyers & Legal Professionals. Unpublished study.

69   Saunderson (2016).

70   Saunderson (2016), 195.

71   Kelly Graves (April 19, 2023). When I was a junior associate, I had a (tedious) assignment to summarize a set of deposition transcripts for a partner. LinkedIn. https://www.linkedin.com/posts/kelly-graves-2b6843180_why-its-important-to -show-gratitude-at-workand-activity-7054413146995757056-xy5L/?trk=public _profile_like_view.

72   Sara Algoe (April 16, 2023). Why It's Important to Show Gratitude at Work— and What's the Best Way to Do It. *Wall Street Journal*. https://www.wsj.com /articles/show-gratitude-work-aaf8f20c.

73   Kellerman & Seligman (2023).

74   Isaac Prilleltensky & Ora Prilleltensky (2021). *How People Matter: Why It Affects Health, Happiness, Love, Work and Society*. Cambridge: Cambridge University Press.

75   Morris Rosenberg & Claire B. McCullough (1981). Mattering: Inferred Significance & Mental Health Among Adolescents. 2 *Research on Community & Mental Health*, 163–182.

76   Andrew Reece et al. (2021). Mattering Is an Indicator of Organizational Health and Employee Success. 16(2) *Journal of Positive Psychology*, 228–248.

77   Gail Cornwall (September 27, 2023). Want to Believe in Yourself? 'Mattering' Is Key. *New York Times*. https://www.nytimes.com/2023/09/27/well/mind/mental -health-mattering-self-esteem.html.

78   Ae-Kyung Jung & Mary Heppner (2017). Development and Validation of a Work Mattering Scale (WMS). 25(3) *Journal of Career Assessment*, 467–483.

79   Gordon L. Flett (2018). *The Psychology of Mattering: Understanding the Human Need to Be Significant*. London: Academic Press. See also Prilleltensky & Prilleltensky (2021), 176.

80   Patrick R. Krill, Nikki Degeneffe, Kelly Ochoki, & Justin J. Anker (2022). People, Professionals, & Profit Centers: The Connection Between Lawyer Well-Being and Employer Values. 12(6) *Behavioral Science*, 177–193.

81   Interview with Dr. Zachary Mercurio, February 21, 2024.

82   Davis & ALM (2023).

83   Kerry Roberts Gibson, Kate O'Leary, & Joseph R. Weintraub (January 23, 2020). The Little Things That Make Employees Feel Appreciated. *Harvard Business Review*. https://hbr.org/2020/01/the-little-things-that-make-employees-feel -appreciated.

84   Flett (2018), 35.

Chapter 4

85 Anja Van den Broeck & Gavin R. Slemp (2023). Leadership: A Self-Determination Theory Perspective. In *The Oxford Handbook of Self-Determination Theory* (Richard M. Ryan, ed.), 920–938. New York: Oxford University Press.

86 Interview with Yvette Ostolaza, February 8, 2024.

87 Frank Martela et al. (2021). What Makes Work Meaningful? Longitudinal Evidence for the Importance of Autonomy and Beneficence for Meaningful Work. *Journal of Vocational Behavior*, 131, Article 103631. See also Anja Van den Broeck, D. Lance Ferris, Chu-Hsiang Chang, & Christopher C. Rosen (2016). A Review of Self-Determination Theory's Basic Psychological Needs at Work. 42(5) *Journal of Management*, 1195–1229.

88 Questions 1–4 are adapted from Jessica Perlo et al. (2017). IHI Framework for Improving Joy in Work. IHI White Paper. Cambridge, MA: Institute for Healthcare Improvement, 18. The rest are my own based on the autonomy categories.

89 Martela et al. (2021).

90 Charlie Gilkey (2023). *Team Habits: How Small Actions Lead to Extraordinary Results*. New York: Hachette Book Group.

91 Scott Tannenbaum & Eduardo Salas (2021). *Teams That Work: The Seven Drivers of Team Effectiveness*. New York: Oxford University Press.

92 Mercurio et al. (2024).

93 David Cross (January 27, 2024). Yesterday we ended the third week of the most intense trial I've had in my career—with a few days still to go next week. LinkedIn. https://www.linkedin.com/posts/david-cross-5176b76_magic-grits -activity-7157138141320015872-Srp6/.

94 Brian Elliott (May 15, 2024). Well-structured hashtag#hybrid programs focus on moments that matter. LinkedIn. https://www.linkedin.com/posts/belliott _hybrid-hybrid-hybrid-activity-7196543951695147008-ktO0/.

95 Karen A. John & Priti Pradhan Shah (1997). Interpersonal Relationships and Task Performance: An Examination of Mediating Processes in Friendship and Acquaintance Groups. 72(4) *Journal of Personality and Social Psychology*, 775–790.

96 Tom Rath (2006). *Vital Friends: The People You Can't Afford to Live Without*. New York: Gallup Press.

97 Zachary Mercurio, Ph.D. (November 16, 2022). How to Create Mattering at Work. LinkedIn. https://www.linkedin.com/pulse/how-create-mattering-work -zach-mercurio-ph-d-/.

98 Avik Basu, Jason Duvall, & Rachel Kaplan (2018). Attention Restoration Theory: Exploring the Role of Soft Fascination and Mental Bandwidth. *Environment and Behavior*, 1–27.

99 Shelly L. Gable & Harry T. Reis (2010). Good News! Capitalizing on Positive Events in an Interpersonal Context. 42 *Advances in Experimental Social*

Psychology, 195–257. See also Shelly L. Gable, Gian C. Gonzaga, & Amy Strachman (2006). Will You Be There for Me When Things Go Right? Supportive Responses to Positive Event Disclosures. 91(5) *Journal of Personality and Social Psychology*, 904–917; Shelly L. Gable & Courtney L. Gosnell (2011). The Positive Side of Close Relationships. In *Designing Positive Psychology: Taking Stock and Moving Forward* (Kennon M. Sheldon, Todd B. Kashdan, & Michael F. Steger, eds.), 265–279. New York: Oxford University Press.

100 Remus Ilies, Joyce E. Bono, & Arnold B. Bakker (2024). Crafting Well-Being: Employees Can Enhance Their Own Well-Being by Savoring, Reflecting upon, and Capitalizing on Positive Work Experiences. 11 *Annual Review of Organizational Psychology and Organizational Behavior*, 63–91. See also Remus Ilies, Jessica Keeney, & Zen W. Goh (2015). Capitalising on Positive Work Events by Sharing Them at Home. 64(3) *Applied Psychology*, 578–598.

101 Ilies, Keeney, & Goh (2015). See also Remus Ilies et al. (2007). When Can Employees Have a Family Life? The Effects of Daily Workload and Affect on Work-Family Conflict and Social Activities at Home. 92 *Journal of Applied Psychology*, 1368–1379.

102 Microsoft Work Trend Index (September 22, 2022). *Hybrid Work Is Just Work. Are We Doing It Wrong?* https://www.microsoft.com/en-us/worklab/work-trend -index/hybrid-work-is-just-work#:~:text=2%20out%20of%203%20 employees,tool%20for%20your%20leadership%20layer.

103 World Economic Forum (May 2023). *Future of Jobs Report 2023: Insight Report.* https://www3.weforum.org/docs/WEF_Future_of_Jobs_2023.pdf.

104 Gallup (2023). *State of the Global Workplace.* New York: Gallup Press.

105 The Best Companies for Future Leaders (December 2023). *Time.* https://time .com/collection/best-companies-for-future-leaders/.

106 Jens Baier et al. (June 13, 2024). *How Work Preferences Are Shifting in the Age of GenAI.* Decoding Global Talent. Boston Consulting Group. https://www.bcg .com/publications/2024/how-work-preferences-are-shifting-in-the-age-of-genai.

107 Ling Li (2022). Reskilling and Upskilling the Future-Ready Workforce for Industry 4.0 and Beyond. *Information Systems Frontiers*, 1–16. https://doi.org /10.1007/s10796-022-10308-y.

108 While I will mention certain studies specifically, the work in this section stems largely from Albert Bandura. To learn more about the types and nuances of efficacy, please read Albert Bandura (1997). *The Exercise of Control.* New York: Freeman.

109 Kotaro Shoji et al. (2015). Associations Between Job Burnout and Self-Efficacy: A Meta-Analysis. 29(4) *Anxiety, Stress, & Coping*, 367–386. See also Mercedes Ventura, Marisa Salanova, & Susan Llorens (2015). Professional Self-Efficacy as a Predictor of Burnout and Engagement: The Role of Challenge and Hindrance Demands. 149(3) *Journal of Psychology*, 277–302.

110 Albert Bandura (2000). Exercise of Human Agency Through Collective Efficacy. 9(3) *Current Directions in Psychological Science*, 75–78.

111 Richard M. Ryan & Edward L. Deci (2017). *Self-Determination Theory: Basic Psychological Needs in Motivation, Development, and Wellness.* New York: Guilford Press, chap. 20: Motivation and Need Satisfaction in Video Games and Virtual Environments, 508–531. See also Jane McGonigal (2015). *SuperBetter: The Power of Living Gamefully.* New York: Penguin Books, 131–158.

112 Green (2023).

113 World Economic Forum (2023), 7.

114 World Economic Forum (2023), 42.

115 Noguera Lasa et al. (2024).

Chapter 5

116 Baier et al. (2024).

117 Francesco Montani & Veronique Deganais-Desmarais (2018). Unraveling the Relationship Between Role Overload and Organizational Citizenship Behavior: A Test of Mediating and Moderating Effects. 36(6) *European Management Journal*, 757–768. See also Van den Broeck & Slemp (2023).

118 Shu-Ling Chen, Chih-Ting Shih, & Nai-Wen Chi (2018). A Multi-Level Job Demands-Resources Model of Work Engagement: Antecedents, Consequences, & Boundary Conditions. 31(5) *Human Performance*, 282–304.

119 YMCA WorkWell (2022).

120 Heidi K. Gardner & Ivan A. Matviak (2022). *Smarter Collaboration: A New Approach to Breaking Down Barriers and Transforming Work.* Boston: Harvard Business Review Press.

121 Rose Hollister & Michael D. Watkins (September–October 2018). Too Many Projects. *Harvard Business Review.*

122 Gardner & Matviak (2022), 238.

123 For a complete list of questions, see Hollister & Watkins (2018), 69.

124 Annie Dean (Global Head of Team Anywhere at Atlassian) (April 2, 2024). We've outgrown the office as a way to share knowledge. LinkedIn. https://www .linkedin.com/posts/anniedeanzaitzeff_weve-outgrown-the-office-as-a-way-to -share-activity-7180987774987063296-TmpI/.

125 You can read more about the Mindful Business Charter and see the complete language for each pillar here: https://www.mindfulbusinesscharter.com/the -charter.

126 Interview with Ben Carpenter, February 5, 2024. See also Jessica Cherry (October 27, 2023). Fostering Attorney Well-Being by Humanizing Attorney-Client Relationships: The Mindful Business Charter & U.S. Bank Well-Being Guidelines Offer Pathways to Change. *Practical Law.* https://static1.squarespace .com/static/5e6d105ff4b7d15cf766c1e1/t/654a88cd56fdd568d0dedead /1699383503253/MBC+and+US+BANK.pdf.

127   Interview with Michael S. Kraut, May 6, 2024.

128   Tannenbaum & Salas (2021).

129   Tannenbaum & Salas (2021), 126–127.

130   Davis & ALM (2023).

131   Daniel C. Ganster, Christopher C. Rosen, & Gwenith G. Fisher (2018). Long Working Hours and Well-Being: What We Know, What We Do Not Know, and What We Need to Know. 33 *Journal of Business Psychology*, 25–39.

132   Laura M. Giurge & Kaitlin Woolley (2022). Working During Non-Standard Work Time Undermines Intrinsic Motivation. 170 *Organizational Behavior and Human Decision Processes*, Article 104134.

133   Giurge & Woolley (2022).

134   Microsoft Work Trend Index (May 9, 2023). *Will AI Fix Work?* https://sunrise.co /wp-content/uploads/2023/09/WTI_Will_AI_Fix_Work_2023.pdf.

135   Microsoft Work Trend Index (2023).

136   Dan Schawbel (August 6, 2024). Most Employees Say AI Is Adding to Their Workload—Here's How Leaders Can Help. *Workplace Intelligence Weekly*. LinkedIn. https://www.linkedin.com/pulse/most-employees-say-ai-adding -workload-heres-how-leaders-dan-schawbel-q17je/.

137   Microsoft Work Trend Index (2024). *AI at Work Is Here: Now Comes the Hard Part*. https://www.microsoft.com/en-us/worklab/work-trend-index/ai-at-work-is -here-now-comes-the-hard-part.

138   Schawbel (2024).

139   The presentation I heard was given by Helen Fanucci at a Senior Executive Network meeting in Kansas City, MO, on May 16, 2024. Helen was referencing a public LinkedIn post by Wendy Haddad, a senior leader at Microsoft.

140   Hollister & Watkins (2018), 71.

141   Atlassian (n.d.). Meet the #1 Barrier to Productivity. *Work Life* (blog). https:// www.atlassian.com/blog/workplace-woes-meetings.

142   Atlassian (2023). *Lessons Learned: 1,000 Days of Distributed at Atlassian*. https://atlassianblog.wpengine.com/wp-content/uploads/2024/01 /lessonslearned.pdf.

Chapter 6

143   David M. Fisher & Jennifer M. Ragsdale (2019). The Importance of Definitional and Temporal Issues in the Study of Resilience. 68(4) *Applied Psychology: An International Review*, 583–620. See also David Fletcher and Mustafa Sarkar (2013). Psychological Resilience: A Review and Critique of Definitions, Concepts, and Theory. 18(1) *European Psychologist*, 12–23.

144   Ann S. Masten (2001). Ordinary Magic: Resilience Processes in Development. 56(3) *American Psychologist*, 227–238. See also Carolyn Youssef and Fred Luthans (2007). Positive Organizational Behavior in the Workplace: The Impact of Hope, Optimism, and Resilience. 33 *Journal of Management*, 774–800.

145   Alexis Jeannotte, Erin Eatough, & Gabriella Rosen Kellerman (2020). *Resilience in an Age of Uncertainty: Cultivating Resilient Leaders, Teams & Organizations.* Better Up Labs.

146   Karen van Dam (2013). Employee Adaptability to Change at Work: A Multidimensional Resource-Based Framework. In *The Psychology of Organizational Change: Part III—Predicting Employees' Reactions to Change: Individual Factors.* (Shaul Oreg, Alexandra Michael, & Rune Todnem By, eds.), 123–142. Cambridge: Cambridge University Press.

147   Brassey et al. (2022).

148   Brassey et al. (2022).

149   Erica Seville (2017). *Resilient Organizations: How to Survive, Thrive, and Create Opportunities Through Crisis and Change.* London: Kogan Page.

150   Charles Duhigg (February 25, 2016). What Google Learned from Its Quest to Build the Perfect Team. *New York Times.* https://www.nytimes.com/2016/02/28/magazine/what-google-learned-from-its-quest-to-build-the-perfect-team.html.

151   Interview with Sarah Dodds-Brown, May 3, 2024.

152   Constantinos G. V. Coutifaris & Adam M. Grant (2022). Taking Your Team Behind the Curtain: The Effect of Leader Feedback-Sharing and Feedback-Seeking on Team Psychological Safety. 33(4) *Organization Science*, 1574–1598.

153   Bradley L. Kirkman & Adam C. Stoverink (2023). *Unbreakable: Building and Leading Resilient Teams.* Stanford, CA: Stanford University Press.

154   Bradley L. Kirkman & Adam C. Stoverink (2021). Building Resilient Virtual Teams. 50(1) *Organizational Dynamics*, Article 100825. See also Adam C. Stoverink, Bradley L. Kirkman, Sal Mistry, & Benson Rosen (2020). Bouncing Back Together: Toward a Theoretical Model of Work Team Resilience. 45(2) *Academy of Management Review*, 395–422.

155   K. M. Sharika, Swarag Thaikkandi, Nivedita, & Michael L. Platt (2024). Interpersonal Heart Rate Synchrony Predicts Effective Information Processing in a Naturalistic Group Decision-Making Task. 121(21) *Proceedings of the National Academy of Sciences*, Article e2313801121.

156   George M. Alliger, Christopher P. Cerasoli, Scott I. Tannenbaum, & William B. Vessey (2015). Team Resilience: How Teams Flourish Under Pressure. 44 *Organizational Dynamics*, 176–184.

157   Richard J. Davidson & Sharon Begley (2012). *The Emotional Life of Your Brain. How Its Unique Patterns Affect the Way You Think, Feel, and Live—and How You Can Change Them.* New York: Penguin Group.

158 All of the information in this section comes from Atlassian (June 2024) *State of Teams 2024*. https://www.atlassian.com/blog/state-of-teams-2024?utm_source=linkedin&utm_medium=pai%5B%E2%80%A6%5D%257CF:awareness%257CI:state-of-teams-2024-anniedean-linkedin%257C.

159 Patrick Guggenberger et al. (April 26, 2023). *The State of Organizations 2023: Ten Shifts Transforming Organizations*. McKinsey & Company. https://www.mckinsey.com/capabilities/people-and-organizational-performance/our-insights/the-state-of-organizations-2023#/.

160 Guggenberger et al. (2023), 6.

161 Guggenberger et al. (2023), 11.

162 Jennifer A. Chatman, David F. Caldwell, Charles A. O'Reilly, & Bernadette Doerr (2014). Parsing Organizational Culture: How the Norm for Adaptability Influences the Relationship Between Culture Consensus and Financial Performance in High-Technology Firms. 35 *Journal of Organizational Behavior*, 785–808.

163 Chatman et al. (2014), 797–803.

164 Jeannotte, Eatough, & Kellerman (2020).

165 Guggenberger et al. (2023), 12.

166 Edwine Barasa, Rahab Mbau, & Lucy Gilson (2018). What Is Resilience and How Can It Be Nurtured? A Systematic Review of Empirical Literature on Organizational Resilience. 7(6) *International Journal of Health Policy Management*, 491–503.

167 Seville (2017), 20.

168 Michelle A. Barton, Marlys Christianson, Christopher G. Myers, & Kathleen Sutcliffe (2020). Resilience in Action: Leading for Resilience in Response to COVID-19. 4(3) *BMJ Leader*, 117–119.

169 Jonathan Thomas (2023). *Intentional Interruptions: Learning to Be Interrupted the Way God Intended*. Fearne, Scotland: Christian Focus Publications.

170 Michelle A. Burton & William A. Kahn (2019). Group Resilience: The Place and Meaning of Relational Pauses. 40(9) *Organization Studies*, 1409–1429.

171 Arnold B. Bakker, Evangelia Demerouti, & Ana Sanz-Vergel (2023). Job Demands-Resources Theory: Ten Years Later. 10 *Annual Review of Organizational Psychology and Organizational Behavior*, 25–53. See also Wilmar B. Schaufeli et al. (2002). The Measurement of Burnout and Engagement: A Two Sample Confirmatory Factor Analytic Approach. 3 *Journal of Happiness Studies*, 71–92.

172 Bakker, Demerouti, & Sanz-Vergel (2023).

173 Parul Malik & Pooja Garg (2017). Learning Organization and Work Engagement: The Mediating Role of Employee Resilience. 31(8) *International Journal of Human Resource Management*, 1071–1094.

174 Ludmila Kasparkova, Martin Vaculik, Jakub Prochazka, & Wilmar B. Schaufeli (2018). Why Resilient Workers Perform Better: The Roles of Job Satisfaction and Work Engagement. 33(1) *Journal of Workplace Behavioral Health*, 43–62.

175 Adedapo Oluwaseyi Ojo, Olawole Fawehinmi, & Mohd Yusoff Yusliza (2021). Examining the Predictors of Resilience and Work Engagement During the COVID-19 Pandemic. 13(5) *Sustainability*, Article 2902.

Chapter 7

176 Interview with Natalie Archibald, August 30, 2024.

177 Michael F. Steger & Bryan J. Dik (2010). Work as Meaning: Individual and Organizational Benefits of Engaging in Meaningful Work. In *Oxford Handbook of Positive Psychology and Work* (P. Alex Linley, Susan Harrington, & Nicola Garcea, eds.), 131–142. New York: Oxford University Press.

178 This definition is a combination from the work of Brené Brown and Kelly McGonigal. See Brené Brown (2018). *Dare to Lead*. New York: Random House; and Kelly McGonigal (2015). *The Upside of Stress*. New York: Avery.

179 Blake A. Allan, Ryan D. Duffy, & Brian Collisson (2018). Helping Others Increases Meaningful Work: Evidence from Three Experiments. 65(2) *Journal of Counseling Psychology*, 155–165.

180 Allan, Duffy, & Collisson (2018).

181 Christine L. Porath, Cristina B. Gibson, & Gretchen M. Spreitzer (2022). To Thrive or Not to Thrive: Pathways for Sustaining Thriving at Work. 42 *Research in Organizational Behavior*, 1–17.

182 Mercurio et al. (2024).

183 Paula Davis (May 19, 2021). Leadership Lessons from a Former F/A-18 Weapons System Officer. Forbes.com. https://www.forbes.com/sites/pauladavis/2021/05/19/leadership-lessons-from-a-former-fa-18-weapons-system-officer/.

184 Teresa Amabile & Steven Kramer (2011). *The Progress Principle: Using Small Wins to Ignite Joy, Engagement, and Creativity at Work*. Boston: Harvard Business Review Press.

185 Rob Cross & Karen Dillon (2023). *The Microstress Effect: How Little Things Pile Up and Create Big Problems—and What to Do About It*. Boston: Harvard Business Review Press.

186 Gabriele Oettingen (2012). Future Thought and Behavior Change. 23 *European Review of Social Psychology*, 1–63. See also Gabriele Oettingen (2014). *Rethinking Positive Thinking: Inside the New Science of Motivation*. New York: Penguin Group.

187 David L. Cooperrider, Diana Whitney, & Jacqueline M. Stavros (2008). *Appreciative Inquiry Handbook for Leaders of Change*, 2nd ed. Brunswick, OH: Crown Custom.

188   Peter M. Gollwitzer (2014). Weakness of the Will: Is a Quick Fix Possible? 38 *Motivation and Emotion*, 305–322. See also Peter M. Gollwitzer (1999). Implementation Intentions: Strong Effects of Simple Plans. 54 *American Psychologist*, 493–505; and Peter M. Gollwitzer & Paschal Sheeran (2006). Implementation Intentions and Goal Achievement: A Meta-Analysis of Effects and Processes. 38 *Advances in Experimental Social Psychology*, 69–119.

189   Gollwitzer (2014), 306.

190   Thank you to my retired solider friends, Dan Mason and Brent Sicely, for helping me to articulate this concept so I could translate it into nonmilitary speak.

191   Melissa A. Valentine (2014). Informal Peer Interaction & Practice Type as Predictors of Physician Performance on Maintenance of Certification Examinations. 149(6) *JAMA Surgery*, 597–603.

192   Lara B. Aknin & Gillian M. Sandstrom (2024). People Are Surprisingly Hesitant to Reach Out to Old Friends. *Communications Psychology*. https://www.nature .com/articles/s44271-024-00075-8#citeas. See also Jorge Walter, Daniel Z. Levin, & J. Keith Murnigham (2015). Reconnection Choices: Selecting the Most Valuable (vs. Most Preferred) Dormant Ties. 26(5) *Organization Science*, 1447–1465.

193   Dawn Klinghoffer, Karen Kocher, & Natalie Luna (June 5, 2024). Onboarding New Employees in a Hybrid Workplace. *Harvard Business Review*. https://hbr .org/2024/06/onboarding-new-employees-in-a-hybrid-workplace.

194   Bill Schaninger, Bryan Hancock, & Emily Field (2023). *Power to the Middle: Why Managers Hold the Keys to the Future of Work*. Boston: Harvard Business Review Press.

195   Emma Seppälä & Marissa King (June 29, 2017). Burnout at Work Isn't Just About Exhaustion. It's Also About Loneliness. *Harvard Business Review*. https://hbr .org/2017/06/burnout-at-work-isnt-just-about-exhaustion-its-also-about -loneliness.

196   Mercurio et al. (2024).

197   Kelly McGonigal writes about bigger-than-self goals in her wonderful book *The Upside of Stress*; see McGonigal (2015), 143–151.

198   Justin M. Berg, Amy Wrzesniewski, & Jane E. Dutton (2010). Perceiving and Responding to Challenges in Job Crafting at Different Ranks: When Proactivity Requires Adaptivity. 13 *Journal of Organizational Behavior*, 158–186. See also Rob Baker (2020). *Personalization at Work: How HR Can Use Job Crafting to Drive Performance, Engagement, and Well-Being*. New York: Kogan Page; and Maria Tims & Arnold B. Bakker (2010). Job Crafting: Towards a New Model of Individual Job Redesign. 36(2) *Journal of Industrial Psychology*, 1–9.

199   Baker (2020), 63–69.

200   Amabile & Kramer (2011).

201   Ilies, Bono, & Bakker (2024).

202 Ilies, Bono, & Bakker (2024), 81.

203 Tait D. Shanafelt et al. (2009). *Career Fit and Burnout Among Academic Faculty*. 169(10) *JAMA Internal Medicine*, 990–995.

204 Baker (2020), 145.

205 Oliver Burkeman (2023). *Four Thousand Weeks: Time Management for Mortals*. London: Picador.

206 Mercurio et al. (2024).

Conclusion

207 Ben Wigert & Heather Barrett (September 6, 2023). The Manager Squeeze: How the New Workplace Is Testing Team Leaders. Gallup. https://www.gallup.com /workplace/510326/manager-squeeze-new-workplace-testing-team-leaders.aspx.

208 Gallup (2024).

209 Kristin Schwab (October 30, 2023). CEO Turnover is Big Right Now. Marketplace. https://www.marketplace.org/2023/10/30/ceo-turnover-increase -great-resignation/. See also Challenger, Gray, & Christmas (October 19, 2023). *CEO Turnover Report*. https://www.challengergray.com/blog/ceo-exits-continue -record-clip-164-ceos-leave-their-posts-in-september-2023-q3-highest-quarterly -total-on-record/.

210 J. Fisher et al. (2024).

211 John A. Bargh et al. (2001). The Automated Will: Nonconscious Activation and Pursuit of Behavioral Goals. 81(6) *Journal of Personality and Social Psychology*, 1014–1027. See also John A. Bargh & Ezequiel Morsella (2008). The Unconscious Mind. 3(1) *Perspectives on Psychological Science*, 73–79.

212 Conversation with Becca Worple on July 11, 2024. I included some additional details from the following blog post: Doug Worple (October 17, 2021). It Was a 17,000 Mile Drive to Get Here. *Farmer Doug Blog*. https://goldendogfarm.com /blogs/thoughts-raised-on-the-farm/it-was-a-17-000-mile-drive-to-get-here.

213 Bakker, Demerouti, & Sanz-Vergel (2023).

Index

Perlo, Jessica, 127n88
perseverance, 90
physicians, 112, 119
plastic injection molding, 1–3
positive feedback, 29, 45, 70
positive work cultures, 21, 26, 28, 36
positive workplace experiences,
  63–65, 118
post-traumatic growth (PTG), 6
prevention, burnout, 3–4, 32–35
PRIMED model, 91–92, 105
priming, 123–24
problem solving, 110
productive disruptions, 103
productivity, 21, 31, 48, 90; GenAI
  and, 84; resilience and, 100
professional development, 35–36,
  53–54. *See also* career development
programming, 36–38, 66, 69, 79;
  certificate, 53–54, 67; EAPs, 35, 63;
  executive education, 53–54;
  recognition, 45
psychology, 3–5, 7, 9–10, 30, 62–63,
  123; of mattering, 49–50; of
  motivation, 32, 47; of safety, 80, 92,
  94–96
purpose, 93. *See also* meaning,
  sense of

quality of life, 82
quantification, 110
"quiet quitting," 17

Reciprocity Effect (nonprofit), 43
recognition, 43, 118; appreciation
  and, 21, 44–49; lack of, 29–31,
  44–45; sticky, 9–10, 45–52
recruitment, 51–52, 66
relational pauses, 103–4
relationship building, 2–3, 57, 60–65,
  77–81, 111–14
remote work, 7, 15–16
resignations, voluntary, 16–17
resilience, 1–4, 35, 91–95, 121;
  organizational, 100–105; stress

and, 9–10, 89–90, 104; TNTs
  related to, 96–100, 103–5;
  uncertainty and, 89–90, 105
reskilling, upskilling and, 66–68, 70
resources, 34, 57, 75, 97, 100, 115;
  coaching, 54, 66–67, 69, 123
respect, 2–3, 93
responsibilities, 35–39, 57–58, 74,
  96, 115
retention, 16–19, 51–52
return on investment (ROI), 22,
  25, 37
review processes, 34–35
risk, 18
rotation, job, 68

safety, psychological, 80, 92, 94–96
sanitation workers, 43
schedules, 82–84; autonomy in, 56;
  unstructured time in, 61–62
scope of work, 74
self-awareness, 123
self-efficacy, 68, 104
senior leadership, 15, 19, 27, 48–49,
  60–62, 114, 125; limited line
  of sight for, 75; values-based
  behaviors modeled by, 116
Shah, Jay, 15–16
short-term strategies, 4–5, 28, 36
Sidley Austin, LLP, 53–54, 66, 69
silos, workplace, 28, 35–39
situational awareness, 101–2
skill discretion, 34
skills audits, 67
skills gaps, 70
social autonomy, 56
social intelligence, 3
stakeholders, 38
State of Teams report, Atlassian, 98
State of the Global Workplace report
  (Gallup), 65
Staton, Rahan, 43, 52, 135n63
sticky goals, 110–12
sticky recognition, 9–10, 45–52
storytelling, 117

About the Author

Paula Davis, JD, MAPP, is the founder and CEO of the Stress & Resilience Institute. For 15 years, she has been a trusted advisor to leaders in organizations of all sizes, helping them to make work better. Paula is a globally recognized expert on the effects of workplace stress, burnout prevention, workplace well-being, and building resilience for individuals and teams.

Paula left her law practice after seven years and earned a master's degree in applied positive psychology from the University of Pennsylvania. As part of her post-graduate training, Paula was selected to be part of the University of Pennsylvania faculty, teaching and training resilience skills to soldiers as part of the Army's Comprehensive Soldier and Family Fitness program. The Penn team trained resilience skills to more than 40,000 soldiers and their family members.

Paula is the author of *Beating Burnout at Work: Why Teams Hold the Secret to Well-Being and Resilience*, which is about burnout prevention using a teams-based approach. *Beating Burnout at Work* was nominated for best new book by the Next Big Idea Club, which is curated by Adam Grant, Susan Cain, Malcom Gladwell, and Daniel Pink.

Paula has shared her expertise at educational institutions such as Harvard Law School, Wharton School Executive Education, and Princeton. She is a two-time recipient of the distinguished teaching award from the Medical College of Wisconsin.

Her expertise has been featured in and on the *New York Times*, *O, The Oprah Magazine*, the *Washington Post*, and many other media outlets. Paula is also a contributor to *Forbes, Fast Company,* and *Psychology Today.*

Paula's website is www.stressandresilience.com, and you can reach her directly at paula@stressandresilience.com.

About Wharton School Press

Wharton School Press, the book publishing arm of the Wharton School of the University of Pennsylvania, was established to inspire bold, insightful thinking within the global business community.

An imprint of University of Pennsylvania Press, Wharton School Press publishes a select list of award-winning, bestselling, and thought-leading books that offer trusted business knowledge to help leaders at all levels meet the challenges of today and the opportunities of tomorrow. Led by a spirit of innovation and experimentation, Wharton School Press leverages groundbreaking digital technologies and has pioneered a fast-reading business book format that fits readers' busy lives, allowing them to swiftly emerge with the tools and information needed to make an impact. Wharton School Press books offer guidance and inspiration on a variety of topics, including leadership, management, strategy, innovation, entrepreneurship, finance, marketing, social impact, public policy, and more.

To find books that will inspire and empower you to increase your impact and expand your personal and professional horizons, visit *wsp.wharton.upenn.edu.*

About the Wharton School

Founded in 1881 as the world's first collegiate business school, the Wharton School of the University of Pennsylvania is shaping the future of business by incubating ideas, driving insights, and creating leaders who change the world. With a faculty of more than 235 renowned professors, Wharton has 5,000 undergraduate, MBA, executive MBA, and doctoral students. Each year 100,000 professionals from around the world advance their careers through Wharton Executive Education's individual, company-customized, and online programs, and thousands of pre-collegiate students explore business concepts through Wharton's Global Youth Program. More than 105,000 Wharton alumni form a powerful global network of leaders who transform business every day.

www.wharton.upenn.edu

UNIVERSITY OF
PENNSYLVANIA
PRESS

About Penn Press

True to its Philadelphia roots, Penn Press is well-known for its distinguished list of publications in American history and culture, including innovative work on the transnational currents that surrounded and shaped the republic from the colonial period through the present, as well as prize-winning publications in urban studies. The Press is equally renowned for its publications in European history, literature, and culture from late antiquity through the early modern period. Penn Press's social science publications tackle contemporary political issues of concern to a broad readership of citizens and scholars, notably including a long-standing commitment to publishing path-breaking work in international human rights. Penn Press also publishes outstanding works in archaeology, economic history, business, and Jewish Studies in partnership with local institutions.

You can learn more about our recent publications by visiting www.pennpress.org or viewing our seasonal catalogs.

Printed in the USA
CPSIA information can be obtained
at www.ICGtesting.com
JSHW081945031224
73972JS00002B/1

9 781613 631898